Richard Andrew
Called to Paint

THE 104TH INFANTRY, 26TH DIVISION, A.E.F.
General Passaga Decorating the Colors at Boucq, France, April 28, 1918
From the mural painting by Richard Andrew

Boston Herald
Sunday, February 4, 1934

Richard Andrew
Called to Paint

Marian G. Mullet: Author
Martha M. Winsor: Researcher and Editor
Deborah W. Batt: Photographer and Graphic Designer

Langdon Street Press
212 3rd Avenue North, Suite 290
Minneapolis, MN 55401
612.455.2293
www.langdonstreetpress.com

ISBN - 978-1-934938-91-1
ISBN - 1-934938-91-2
LCCN - 2010924271

Printed in the United States of America

LANGDON
STREET PRESS

Dedicated to the artist, Richard Andrew, who inspired us.

Familiarly called "Dickie" everywhere except to his face;
His rosary is the spinal vertebrae;
His conception of anatomy profound.
A proficient etcher, he dips his tongue in nitric acid,
The better to spray unwary worms with vitriolic questions.

But, when he takes a pencil or brush in his hand,
A spell is woven;
Newcomers approach on tiptoe;
Time pauses,
Gravity is suspended and we are lifted up,
So that ambitions are renewed, and art,
For a moment, seems important and plausible.

Written by students of Richard Andrew for the
1931 Annual Yearbook Faculty Notes,
Mass Art/Massachusetts Normal School of Art Archives

Caricature of Richard Andrew, Instructor
Massachusetts Normal School 1926 Yearbook, MassArt Archives

Acknowledgements

We wish first to acknowledge our immediate family members who traveled with us every day for the last two years as we searched for the art of Richard Andrew and information about his life. They supported and critiqued and participated in every stage of this adventure. Daniel Batt lent us his photographic and artistic assistance. Martin Winsor who assisted in editing and research. Frank Mullet shared his humor, the dining room, and thoughtful reflections with the author as this book became a reality.

Next, we appreciate the extended family of Richard Andrew who contributed their art and memories. We were welcomed in every way into the homes of these warm, intelligent and enthusiastic family members. Their care and preservation of Richard Andrew's artworks has made this book possible. They include Andrew J. Dean, Christopher Dean, Robert C. and Nancy Dean, James C. Dean, Charles E. Dean, Margaret Dean Hurley, Karen Kimball , Nancy and George MacNeil, Cynthia and Tom Adams, Kimberly Lathrop, Linda MacNeil and Dan Dailey, Mark and Kathy Paris, Elizabeth Calabrese, Scott Goddard, and James G. Mullet. Stephen B. Goddard, lifelong journalist and author, provided enthusiastic support in all phases of this book. We give thanks to David Brodeur, Paul Brodeur, and Stephen Brodeur, friends of Richard and Lucy Andrew. They shared their works of art by Richard Andrew and their memories of old family friendships.

Along the way, various archivists, historians, and art experts shared their knowledge and services, and to them we are most appreciative. So many assisted us, and it is very important to us to recognize those whose professional services to this piece of art history has been most significant. They are Susan Greendyke Lachevre: Massachusetts State House Art Collections Manager; Melissa Bateman: Furman University Art Collections Manager; Mabel Bates and Karen Jason of Bridgewater State College; Paul Dobbs: Archivist at MassArt; Stephanie Buck: the librarian at the Cape Ann Historical Association who led us to the Brodeur family; Mary Anderson: Anderson Fine Art Gallery; Carol Miles: Archivist at The Scituate Historical Society; Michael H. Lally: Executive Director of the Whistler House Museum of Art, Lowell, Massachusetts; Stephen Elliott: President of the New York State Historical Association (NYSHA) and Fenimore Art Museum, Cooperstown, New York; Paul D'Ambrosio: Vice President and Curator at NYSHA; Milo Stewart: retired Vice President at NYSHA, and his wife, Ruth; Christine Podmaniczky and Bethany Engel at the Brandywine Museum; and Betsy Wyeth. Thanks to Jonathan Berecz for sharing his expertise in lighting and photography. A special recognition and appreciation is made to Dr. Henry Adams, Chairman of the Art History Department at Case Western University, who wrote the foreword to our book.

We wish to add the names of others who have contributed their Richard Andrew artworks: Richard Davies, James De Angelis, and James Moore. We also give thanks to Kathy and Jim Turner for their warm welcome into the home that Richard Andrew originally designed and built for his wife, Lucy, in Gloucester, Massachusetts.

Lastly, we wish to thank Richard Andrew for bringing family and friends together, many years after his death, in search of his art and the story of his life. The adventure has been incredibly rewarding.

TABLE OF CONTENTS

FOREWORD

Richard Andrew's self-portrait in the Brandywine Museum makes one hold one's breath with wonder and fascination—partly because of its breathtaking technical accomplishment, and partly because it's hard not to become engrossed by the action of the artist. He reaches towards us—right at us, in fact—just at the moment when his loaded brush is about to touch the canvas—the glassy picture plane before our eyes. The painting is dramatic, even a bit confrontational, as well as a wonderful view into the mysteries of picture-making, a glimpse into the process by which brush-strokes and blobs of pigment magically coalesce into a compelling image.

Making a so-called realistic painting is an odder and more difficult business than may at first appear, as anyone who tries to paint quickly learns to his chagrin. Richard Andrew was a master of the craft. Beginners tend to portray what they know is there rather than what they actually see, and to reduce things to hard outlines. A skilled painter knows that he shouldn't inscribe hard outlines but should focus instead on the light that floats around them—that is to say, attempt to freeze the fleeting highlights and shadows on the form, whose patterns change entirely with the slightest shift of position, and do so with firm decisive brushstrokes, so that the clumps of pigment form pleasing, resolute shapes.

Part of what's fascinating about Andrew's self-portrait is that it retains the quality of a sketch, of something still in the process of being formed. In places the brushstrokes seem to float ambiguously, like an image slightly out of focus; but in the key passage of dramatic intensity—where the artist's eyes intently study the reflection in the mirror, calculating how to reduce what he sees to another blob of paint—Andrew sharpens up his brushwork to intensify the focus. What's captivating is the way that Andrew records the excitement and psychological tension of this struggle to make a painting. It's almost as though the image is being created while we watch.

How could I have missed a painter of this skill, a figure who was a worthy peer of Frank Weston Benson, John Singer Sargent, Edmund Tarbell, Charles Hopkinson, and other notables of the Boston School? For I must confess that Richard Andrew was unknown to me before I was shown the mock-up of this book. There are doubtless a variety of reasons for this, but perhaps the largest one is that Andrew was a traditionalist and an idealist when being so was out of fashion. He continued the modes of the 1890s into the 1950s, painting in the manner of John Singer Sargent and Jean-Paul Laurens in an age when Abstract Expressionism was in vogue. Andrew was born in 1869, just shortly after the close of the Civil War, and, somewhat ironically, the same year as the modernist impresario, Alfred Stieglitz. He died in 1956, in the age of the atomic bomb and just before the Soviets launched their first Sputnik into outer space. He was in his twenties in the 1890s, the decade of the Chicago World's Fair, the City Beautiful movement of gleaming white classical architecture and ambitious, uplifting mural projects. Throughout his life he carried forward the idealism of that decade.

Perhaps because he was out of sync with his time, it was clearly a struggle to make a living, and for the central portion of his career, from 1901 to 1937, he devoted much of his time to teaching art, a commitment which surely cut down his artistic productivity. Yet Richard Andrew's paintings and drawings are quite remarkable, and thus it's exciting to discover a study such as this—a true work of love—which brings together his accomplishments in one place and honors his achievements.

Richard Andrew grew up and was schooled in Boston. He received his first serious art training at the Boston Normal Art School, from which he graduated at the age of twenty-four. He then went to Paris for three years, where he studied under the academic masters Jean-Leon Gerome and Jean Paul Laurens at the *Ecole des Beaux-Arts*. And he also took classes at the Academie Julian, where the emphasis was on careful, accurate drawing from the model, and where nothing slipshod was tolerated. Modernism meant Impressionism, which was cautiously accepted as long as it was balanced by careful drawing, but the wilder *-isms* of modern art had not yet exploded into public consciousness. Andrew earnestly absorbed the methods and ideals of his masters. His style was fully formed by the time he became aware of the challenge posed by modern art, which assaulted everything that was traditional, beautifully crafted, or expressive of noble ideals.

For most of his career he supported himself as a teacher. In 1901, age thirty-two, a few years after his return to Boston, he began teaching at the Boston Normal School, from which he retired in 1937, at the age of sixty-eight. His great forte was knowledge of figure drawing and anatomy: his students joked that "his rosary is the spinal vertebrae." His remarkable knowledge of anatomy is evident in his figure drawings, several of which are reproduced in this book. One of my favorites, showing a hand resting on a leg, reveals a masterful understanding of the complex turns of wrist and finger joints, and of the peculiar shapes that come together in a kneecap. He had several notable students, including the great illustrator N. C. Wyeth, one of the giants of American art, and his daughter Henriette.

While he painted landscapes, with a few exceptions Andrew's best paintings and drawings portray the human figure. On the whole, he was most successful in capturing the likeness of men. Something about their hardness suited the careful exactitude of his approach, in which one can catch an echo of the stubborn hard-fisted intensity of his Scottish forbears.

As is often the case with artists, his early works have an earnestness and intensity that is very moving. One can sense his determination to achieve perfect mastery of his craft. One of the best is a likeness of his father, *John Andrew* (1909), a skilled cabinetmaker, in which one can sense the man's integrity, intensity, idealism, and touch of stubbornness. Another masterwork is a portrait of his youngest brother, Nathaniel, titled *The Football Player* (1905), which achieves its impact by its very literalness, and is strikingly similar to a painting of the same general subject by Grant Wood. What is poignant about the painting is the way it jolts our sense of time. Football is a very American game and the schoolboy costume of the player is definitely that of the 1920s. But the solemn sobriety of the effect, with its tall figure clad in black has the feeling of an old master. It might have been executed in the 17th century, by some contemporary of Velasquez. While he was clearly aware of Impressionism, Andrew seldom allowed the form to entirely dissolve in light. His furthest venture in this direction is a lovely canvas of a little girl holding a Japanese lantern, a subject perhaps inspired by a well-known canvas by Sargent. Her face is suffused with red glow, while her fingers, back-lit against the lantern, become strange blue shadows. Even in a case such as this, however, one senses Andrew's determination to capture the visual world accurately, rather than to engage in self-indulgent expressionism.

Around 1912 he made several murals, such as *Autumn* which transports a classical pastoral scene to modern times on the bank of a New England River. The grandest commission of his career came roughly a decade later, when he was commissioned to produce a mural at the Massachusetts State House to honor the 104th Massachusetts Infantry, which performed with great distinction in the First World War. The murals have two sections: one wall devoted to the First World War, which he completed in 1927, and another long wall of murals recording the earlier history of the regiment, which he completed in 1931.

In the best tradition of academic mural painting, as exemplified by his French teacher Jean-Paul Laurens, Andrew's process of designing the painting was extremely thorough. One of the delights of this book is that it reproduces a great many of his working drawings, and thus enables one to see the careful attention he devoted to every face, every hand, and every detail. For the figure of Joan of Arc he even made a careful and detailed clay model over two feet high, a notable work of sculpture in its own right.

Each figure was sensitively characterized. In the World War I scene, for example, there is something marvelously stylish, almost feminine, about the grace of the French officer—as is evident in his costume, the turn of his head, and his aristocratic stance - which artfully contrasts with the blunter, more forceful, more rough-and-ready character of the Americans. For the figure of Joan of Arc he put considerable effort into locating a suitable model, dismissing a bevy of lovely flappers who looked too American, and choosing a girl of French descent, with a solid, well-rounded figure more in keeping with the saint's character. Today, in an era of morally ambiguous, even misguided wars, Andrew's idealism strikes a slightly discordant note. But this note of discord is what makes the painting interesting. It's nice to remember that patriotism was once a virtue, and that wars were once fought for noble motives.

There's no need to enumerate all of Andrew's notable accomplishments, since this book performs this task very nicely, but it seems fitting to close with his self-portrait in the Whistler House Museum in Lowell, Massachusetts. Painted in 1933 when he was sixty-four, it shows a solidly built man, looking back over his shoulder, seen *contre jour* against two windows in the background. There's a tightness to his mouth that suggests both resolution and disappointment. His eyes are wary, appraising. Nothing indicates his role as an artist; tellingly, he titled it simply *Self-portrait*. But at the deepest level this is surely a portrait of his career as an artist, a kind of summing up of both his triumphs and defeats. Without slipping into self-pity, Andrew clearly recognized that he was pushing against the main artistic forces of his age: that his love of craftsmanship, beauty, and close observation of the real world was no longer in fashion. One also senses that he felt he had no choice but to stick to the values he believed in. In front of works such as this one can't help but think of a tag that Andrew's students attached to him, in a yearbook of 1931, to describe his teaching. As they said of his classes, "Art, for a moment, seems important and plausible." Without hesitation, the very same can also be said of many of his paintings, including this one, with its arresting directness and sincerity. Had he been born a few decades earlier, Andrew would probably be better known today. But by the same token it is the conviction with which he held to his artistic ideals, despite the changing mores of his time and place, which makes his work so memorable and poignant.

HENRY ADAMS
Professor of American Art
Case Western Reserve University

HENRY ADAMS

Henry Adams has been singled out by Art News as one of the foremost experts in the American field, and his most recent book, *Eakins Revealed*, has stirred up widespread discussion and controversy. The art historian Robert Rosenblum has said that it possesses "the page-turning momentum of a detective story," while the painter Andrew Wyeth has declared that it is "without doubt the most extraordinary biography I have ever read on an artist."

A graduate of Harvard University, Adams received his M.A. and Ph.D from Yale where he received the Frances Blanshard Prize for the best doctoral dissertation in art history. In 1985 he received the Arthur Kingsley Porter Prize of the College Art Association, the first time this had been awarded to an Americanist or a Museum Curator. In 1989 William Jewell College awarded him its distinguished service medal for his services to Kansas City and the Midwest. In 2001 he received the Northern Ohio Live Visual Arts Award for the best art exhibition of the year in Northern Ohio.

Dr. Adams has produced over 230 publications in the American field, including scholarly and popular articles, books, catalogues, and exhibitions catalogues. These focus principally on American artists of the nineteenth and early twentieth century and include pieces on George Caleb Bingham, Thomas Cole, John F. Kensett, John La Farge, William Morris Hunt, Winslow Homer, Thomas Eakins, George Bellows, Charles Burchfield, Thomas Hart Benton, John Steuart Curry, John Graham, Fairfield Porter, and David Hockney. His books include *John La Farge*, 1987, *Thomas Hart Benton: An American Original*, 1989, *Thomas Hart Benton: Drawing from Life*, 1990, *Albert Bloch: The American Blue Rider*, 1997, *Viktor Schreckengost and 20th-Century Design*, 2000, *Eakins Revealed*, 2005, and *Andrew Wyeth: Master Drawings from the Artist's Collection*, 2006.

Dr. Adams has served as curator of Fine Arts at the Carnegie Museum of Art in Pittsburgh, as curator of American Art at the Nelson-Atkins Museum of Art in Kansas City, as Curator of American Art at the Cleveland Museum of Art, as director of the Cummer Museum of Art in Jacksonville, Florida, and as interim director of the Kemper Museum of Contemporary Art and Design in Kansas City. He has also taught at the University of Illinois, the University of Pittsburgh, Colorado College, The University of Kansas, and the University of Missouri-Kansas City. He currently serves as Professor of American Art at Case Western Reserve University. In 1989, in partnership with film maker Ken Burns, Adams produced a documentary on Thomas Hart Benton which was broadcast nationally on PBS to an audience of 20 million. His book on Thomas Hart Benton will be read from, and featured as a prop, in the forthcoming movie *Prison Song*, featuring Q-tip.

INTRODUCTION: THE ROARING TWENTIES

It was 1924. America radiated confidence. Jobs were plentiful. The stock market roared with increasing profits. Thousands of homes were constructed by young couples who put World War I behind them and thought it was the war to end all wars. Social life boomed with coming-out parties as young women, the darlings of the era called "flappers," danced away, echoing the joy and wonder of the seemingly carefree existence.

Art was in a period of growth and change. Demand for portraiture was diminishing but increasing for photography and Art Deco. John Singer Sargent graced Boston with murals at the Boston Public Library. A major sign of the times was the joint decision by the Massachusetts Legislature and the Massachusetts Art Commission to hold a competition to decorate the Legislative Hall on the third floor of the Massachusetts State House, one of the most important structures in Boston. Erected in 1798, this stately building, designed by architect Charles Bulfinch, would have murals to honor the 104th Massachusetts Infantry Yankee Division.

This book is about Richard Andrew, the winner of that artistic competition and the Massachusetts State House Hall of Valor murals he so beautifully created, and his other artistic works.

Richard Andrew
Boston's Fine American Artist

The Flapper
Subject: Edwina Andrew
Oil on Canvas
31.5 x 49.5 in., c.1925
Private Collection, New Hampshire
(Edwina's story is on page 53.)

PART 1: RICHARD ANDREW: HIS LIFE AND TIMES

Self-portrait: Richard Andrew
Oil on Canvas
18 x 24 in., c. 1890
Private Collection, New Hampshire

Self-portrait
Charcoal and Chalk on Paper
15.5 x 11.5 in.
Private Collection, Boston, Massachusetts

Father of the Artist: John Andrew
Oil on Canvas
19.5 x 23 in.
Private Collection, Norwich, Vermont

BACKGROUND

Richard Andrew has given us a legacy, which has stood straight and tall for more than one hundred years and is one to emulate and put into practice in our own lives. His intelligence, kindness, and devotion to his family and friends were aligned with artistic talents of consummate rank. That he was a fine American artist, there is no doubt. That he was a man of honor and principle, we have learned from his letters, major articles about him, and from those who knew him best. His exceptional work as an art instructor at the Massachusetts Normal School of Art for thirty-six years, and as a Boston artist whose portraits, landscapes, murals, and seascapes traveled throughout the United States and abroad, stands for itself. One need only view his Hall of Valor murals that grace the walls outside of the Legislative Chambers on the third floor of the Massachusetts State House to understand the uncommon stature of the man. The memoirs of Robert C. Dean offer the following historical background:

> The family of Richard Andrew contributed greatly to his strong character. His father, John Andrew, was born on August 12, 1841, at Springburn, Glasgow, Scotland. He lived in Belfast, Ulster, and Glasgow. He was a member of the Royal Grand Black Lodge of Scotland, a religious and political organization that he joined on September 8, 1869, at the age of twenty-eight, in Belfast. When he immigrated to the United States this membership was transferred to the South Boston Lodge.
>
> John Andrew and his family made several business trips to the United States before they settled there permanently. They were in Boston in 1871, Belfast in June of 1873, and in Boston again by September 1873. He and his family returned to Belfast in 1876 and to Scotland in 1877. They finally settled in Boston in 1879 and resided at 27 Wentworth Place. With the difficulties in transporting a family back and forth across the Atlantic Ocean, John and Agnes Andrew demonstrated unusual tenacity and drive to accomplish their goals.
>
> Some of these trips may have been for the purpose of marketing a reversible seat, which he was reputed to have designed for horse-drawn trolley cars. John Andrew disposed of his rights to this invention, which later became standard equipment, though little is known of the details of that transaction. Trolley cars were patented in 1873, marking the beginning of the end of horse and buggy travel. A good cabinetmaker, John was employed for a time in carving church furniture. He had a fine set of cabinetmaker's tools. He also opened a shoe store in Boston, which was run principally by his wife, Agnes.

John Andrew was a distinguished looking man with curly hair and a beard. Richard, the eldest son, painted several portraits of him. Another son, Robert, seemed to bear the strongest likeness to John Andrew. During John's life in Boston, he was an avid gardener and became a friend of Charles Sprague Sargent (1841-1927), who was appointed the Boston Arboretum's first director in 1873, and who shaped the policies and programs of the Arnold Arboretum for fifty-four years. The Arboretum became part of the famous "emerald necklace," the seven-mile-long network of parks of the Boston Parks Department.

John Andrew developed facial cancer, which finally cost him his life on January 21, 1916, when he was seventy-five years old. He is buried at Mt. Auburn Cemetery in Cambridge, Massachusetts.

Agnes Andrew
Oil on Canvas
11.5 x 14 in.
Private Collection, New Hampshire

Robert C. Dean's memoirs also describe the following regarding Richard Andrew's mother, Agnes Morrison. She was born near Belfast, Ireland, the daughter of Railway Superintendent Morrison and his wife, Nancy Elizabeth Potts. Superintendent Morrison was killed by Roman Catholic partisans in January 1846 by being pushed from a railway platform at Malahide Station, the second station north of Dublin. Agnes was then but three weeks old. Later her mother married Schoolmaster Byrne at Kilcrow. They then moved to Belfast. Mr. Byrne became ill and died shortly thereafter. Agnes' mother was a widow for a second time.

Agnes Morrison and John Andrew were married in St. Anne's Church (Protestant), Church of Ireland, Diocese of Connor in Belfast Parish, of Connor, on April 20, 1866, when Agnes was twenty-one. She was at that time employed by a Mr. Jenkins, and as she had bought a dress for £5 on credit, she continued to work for him for three months after her marriage. John Andrew was not pleased. She later pawned the dress for £2, and together with John Andrew's savings of £3 they made a loan to her relative, James Kingsbury, to set him up in business.

Agnes bore nine children with John Andrew, and they lost three of them. Eliza Jane and Nathaniel I died shortly after birth, and Quinten died at the age of twenty-four. Her children worshipped Agnes, and she developed in them strong family loyalty. She helped John Andrew run his store in Boston, and was said to have been the business brains behind its success. There are several portraits of Agnes painted by her son, Richard. Agnes Andrew died on August 5, 1904, and is buried with her husband John in Cambridge, Massachusetts.

Lineage of John and Agnes (Morrison) Andrew

Name	Date of Birth	Place of Birth	Marriage	Death	Notes
John Andrew	Aug. 12, 1841	Springburn, Glasgow, Scotland	April 20, 1866 St. Anne's Belfast Parish Ireland	Jan. 21, 1916 Beachmont Revere, MA	J. Andrew's grandmother buried in the Necropolis Glasgow, Scotland
Agnes Morrison Andrew	Dec. 24, 1945	Near Belfast, Ireland	Same as above	Aug. 5, 1904 Stratford St., West Roxbury, MA	John and Agnes buried in Mt. Auburn Cemetary, Cambridge MA
Children					
Elisa Jane Andrew	Sept. 25, 1867	Belfast, Ireland	N/A	Oct. 22, 1867	Eliza spelled by J. Andrew on Birth Certificate
Richard Andrew	Jan. 9, 1869	Armagh, Near Belfast, Ireland	Lucy Choate Pew Sept. 12, 1905 Gloucester, MA	July 11, 1956 Age 87	Artist Buried in Arlington, MA
John Charles States Andrew	June 15, 1871	61 East Concord St., Boston, MA	Cynthia Elizabeth Hollis - Boston July 29, 1922	July 9, 1955 Age 84	History Professor, Boston Univ. Named for United States
Frederick William Andrew	Sept. 27, 1873	304 West Third St., South Boston, MA	Gertrude, Boston	Dec. 25, 1943 Glen Head, Long Island, NY	Engineer "Fredrick" family spelling
Nathanial James Andrew I	Jan. 27, 1876	Belfast, Ireland	N/A	March 1, 1876	N/A
Minnie Maud Andrew	June 8, 1877	22 Raglam St., Glasgow, Scotland	N/A	Sept. 8, 1966	Raised Robert Andrew's daughters Ruth and Helen
Robert McCammon Andrew	July 6, 1879	Wentworth Blvd., Off Northampton St., Boston, MA	Viola Akeroyd (Div) Tekla (Div) Grace Alspaugh (Div) Josephine Dunlap	June 30, 1949 Forest Hills, Boston	Miner Known as Robert Cameron, named for J.A.'s Uncle Robert McCammon
Quinton David Andrew	April 14, 1882	Colby Place	N/A	June 18, 1906 Boston Hospital	N/A
Nathanial James Andrew II (Buster)	July 17, 1886	Washington St., Boston	Edwina Dobbins (Div) Lorena Johnson	June 30, 1963 Boston	Business Man and Miner

BIRTH AND CHILDHOOD

Richard Andrew, the first-born son of Agnes and John, was born in Armagh, Northern Ireland, near Belfast on January 9, 1869. At that time his parents were planning their move to America. Brief as his childhood experience in Ireland was, he was thankful for the Irish lore and natural beauty that gave him great pleasure. He continued to travel back to Ireland as an adult to paint landscapes.

Richard and his family returned for a two-year stay in Armagh when he was six years old. He said it was the most impressionistic time of his life. During his years in Ireland, he developed a strong sense of this rugged and picturesque country, which he captured in landscape paintings later in his life. His family moved to the United States permanently when Richard was ten years old.

By all accounts, Richard was a sturdy and rather handsome child. His light brown curly hair framed a square face, reflecting his Scottish heritage. People often remarked about his beautiful blue eyes, intense and direct. From his childhood, Richard evidenced an intelligent, determined mind-set, and through these steadfast leanings he showed strong organizational ability and uncommon thoroughness for one so young. According to a February 4, 1934, *Boston Herald* article, Andrew stated, "I started painting and drawing when I was three years old." The term "trustworthy" was often used to describe him throughout his life. Those who interfered with this deeply-focused artist's work risked a display of his impatience. Intense as he was, in terms of his art, Richard's warmth and wit delighted his family, students, and friends.

Elephant
Etching on Paper
Private Collection, San Francisco, California

EARLY EDUCATION

Agnes Andrew was extremely well-read, and she nourished a thirst for learning in her children. Richard applied himself to everything he did and became a fine student. These years of school gave Richard a strong classical education that prepared him for a future in his chosen field of art. His school records qualified him for college admission to the Massachusetts Normal School of Art.

Richard's brothers, John, Charles, and Buster, attended The Boston Latin School. His sister, Minnie Maud, and two nieces, Marguerite and Ruth Andrew, attended The Girls' Latin School. There are no records to verify where Richard Andrew attended grammar school. However, The Boston Latin School certainly influenced the family with its thorough and challenging educational programs.

Boston Latin is the oldest public school in America with a continuous existence. Founded in 1635, it has the distinction of counting five of the signers of the Declaration of Independence among its pupils: John Hancock, Samuel Adams, Benjamin Franklin, Robert Treat Paine, and William Hooper. Its mission statement is "to ground students in a contemporary classical education as preparation for successful college studies, responsible and engaged citizenship, and a rewarding life."

In 1904, Richard Andrew painted a portrait of his brother Buster entitled "The Football Player." The sweater worn in the portrait bears the insignia of The Boston Latin School. This is one of Andrew's most significant paintings. (See Part III, Page 119.)

Photograph: *Richard Andrew,* 1893
Private Collection, Boston, Massachusetts

COLLEGE

In the 1860s, civic and business leaders whose families had made fortunes in the China Trade, textile manufacturing, railroads, and retailing sought to influence the long-term development of Massachusetts. To stimulate learning in technology and fine art, these leaders persuaded the state legislature to found several institutions, including the Massachusetts Institute of Technology (1860) and the Museum of Fine Arts (1870). The third of these, founded in 1873, was the Massachusetts Normal Art School.

Massachusetts Normal School of Art, 1917, Photograph courtesy of MassArt Archives

In 1887, Andrew entered the Massachusetts Normal Art School in Boston, renowned for its preparation of artists and art teachers.

Conditions for admission were as follows:

> Candidates for admission must be over sixteen years of age; must bring a certificate of moral character from some well-known person in the town where they reside; and must present a certificate, or some other evidence, that they have received a grammar-school education or its equivalent.
> Applicants for admission to class A must also pass the examinations of the Normal Art School at the beginning of each school year.
> The subjects in which they are to be examined are as follows:
>   1. Model Drawing (outline)
>   2. Model Drawing (shaded)
>   3. Historic Ornament (outline from east)
> Tuition is free to students residing within the state and intending to teach drawing in public schools, but five dollars per term will be charged for incidentals.

In his years of study at the Normal Art School Richard Andrew received diplomas for classes A, B, C, and D. Class A was devoted to mastering elementary drawing techniques, such as perspective, geometry, projections, building construction, shadowing, and the analysis of styles of historic ornamentation. Class B included drawing and painting with water color and oil. With each medium, lessons included historic schools of design. Class C concentrated on constructive arts (architecture and construction), including plans, elevations, and perspective. This course also focused on machine construction and design, geometry, and wood and iron working in shop. Class D was Modeling and Design in the Round. In this course, the students worked on ornamentation and figure drawing, including portraiture, bas-relief, and casts of all kinds. The only academic coursework he did not take was the public school teacher training curriculum. He worked with many other aspiring artists, and the experience gave him a depth of understanding of his craft. Professional critique of his work was essential to his growth as an artist.

In the June 18, 1892, issue of *Scientific American,* undergraduate Richard Andrew was credited with the design for the statue of Christopher Columbus located at Revere, Massachusetts. The article states: "This monument is Boston's tribute to the great discoverer and is a veritable work of art. It is taken largely from designs drawn by Richard Andrew, a young student of rare promise at the State Normal Art School, Boston." Richard Andrew graduated from The Massachusetts Normal School of Art in 1893 at the age of twenty-four.

ADVANCED STUDIES IN PARIS

Andrew continued his art education and training in Paris from 1893 to 1896 at the Academie Julian and at L'Ecole Des Beaux Arts, studying under Jean Leon Gerome and Jean Paul Laurens at the L'Ecole des Beaux Arts. During his three-year stay in France, this young artist grew emotionally and intellectually by living in Paris and experiencing its beauty and historical importance.

The irresistible charm of Paris gave Richard an appreciation of the French people, business, and politics from the perspective of a citizen. He came to know the City of Light in his travels down broad, tree-lined avenues with their parks and gardens and majestic buildings, the pride of the city. The Eiffel Tower, Cathedral of Notre Dame, Arc de Triomphe, the Louvre Museum, University of Sorbonne, and other architectural marvels became a part of his life. The social life that he experienced in cafés at every street corner, and attending opera and the theater delighted him as he immersed himself in the culture of this great city. Added to his already extensive travels, Richard's experiences in Paris gave him a wealth of knowledge, reflected in his art and teaching for the rest of his life.

The following descriptions of the thorough and challenging opportunities Richard Andrew experienced among the finest artists of the times helps one understand his evolution into a fine artist in his own right.

The Academie Julian was founded by M. Rodolph Julian in 1868 and was located on the Rue de Dragon in the Latin Quarter of Paris. It became one of the best-known private art schools in Paris in the second half of the nineteenth century. The school expanded to five locations throughout France, eventually superseding in prestige L'Ecole des Beaux Arts, the official state art school.

As springtime's blossoms inspired Parisian art students, Richard Andrew studied in the ateliers (studios), walked the halls, and attended lectures and critiques with the likes of other well-known artists who also attended Academie Julian, including Childe Hassam, John Singer Sargent, Thomas Hart Benton, Robert Raushenberg, Cecilia Beaux, Grant Wood, Edmund Tarbell, Mary Cassatt, Frank Weston Benson, and Joseph Henry Sharp. Women were not allowed to attend L'Ecole des Beaux Arts. Even at Academie Julian, they had to pay twice as much for studio space as did men.

Many Americans with art talent trained in France because of the lack of art schools in America. In France and in The Academie Julian's curriculum Modernism influenced artists. The Modernist movement argued that the new realities of the industrial and mechanized age were permanent and imminent, and people should adapt their world view to accept that the new equaled the good, the true, and the beautiful. This philosophy formed the basis of Impressionism, a school of painting that initially focused on work done outdoors (en plein air). Impressionist painting demonstrated that human beings do not see objects, but see light itself.

An important emphasis was on student critiques of each other's work rather than the professor being the all-dominant authority in the classroom. Some of the more famous teachers were William Bougereau, Gustave Boulanger, Jules Lifebure, and Tony Robert Fleury.

From the *History of American Art*, Ingrid Swanson gave an account by Anna Huntington Stanley, who enrolled in 1887. She described the atmosphere as "very disciplined and severe, with not a bit of slipshod drawing tolerated." She wrote that "Boulanger was magnificent, going through the class like a roaring lion, seeing in a glance what you lack in your drawing and he goes for it, holds you up to ridicule for the whole class."

France
Graphite on Paper
8.75 x 6.5 in., c. 1890
Private Collection, Derbyshire, Vermont

L'Ecole des Beaux Arts was organized in 1663 and was for many years the official institution charged with maintaining high fine-art standards in France. Rules included adhering to rigid classical studies, drawing and sculpting from the "antique" models, and following certain rules related to geometric proportion, perspective, and the rendering of anatomy. The school closed in 1793 under chaos caused by rebelling artists. It reopened in 1816 and continues today.

Jean-Paul Laurens (1838 – 1921) was known for his work in the French Academic Style. His work most often focused on historical and religious themes, and his artistic skills were much admired in his time. He is noted for being a teacher of art students from all over the world. Laurens won commissions to paint several public works from the French Third Republic. Most noted were the steel vault of the Paris City Hall and the apse of the Pantheon.

Another of Richard Andrew's esteemed teachers was Jean-Leon Gerome. The Getty Museum website offers the following information: "Born in Vesoul near Switzerland, Gerome's studies finished at sixteen and he began to work under Paul Delarouche, who taught his students the neo-classical style as well as romantic styles, combined in a historical genre. Gerome studied and traveled widely throughout Europe and the Middle East. When he returned in 1844, he entered the atelier (studio) of Charles Gleyre. In 1864, Gerome was appointed as professor to one of three official studios set up by L'Ecole des Beaux Arts. He became a legendary and respected master, noted for his sardonic wit, regimented teaching methods, and extreme hostility to the Impressionists."

Paris Etching
Etching on Paper
c.1890
Private Collection,
Derbyshire, Vermont

The influence of these masters is evident in Richard Andrew's artworks, reflected in the realism and impressionism manifested in his portraits, landscapes, and murals. The rigid classical studies, drawing and sculpting, geometric proportions, perspective, and rendering of anatomy, gave him a thorough knowledge base and the discipline necessary to hone his natural ability.

John Andrew, father of Richard, an immigrant and businessman, must have been very successful in order to highly educate not only Richard but his siblings as well.

Lucy Pew
Oil on Canvas
14.5 x 24.5 in., c.1905
Private Collection, New Hampshire

Becoming Established as an Artist

With Richard's formal art education complete, he established himself as an American artist in 1896 at age twenty-seven. He returned to Boston to practice art in a city where the arts were highly valued and to enjoy his family to whom he was devoted. His mother and father, Agnes and John, were still alive. His sister, Minnie Maud, and his brother, John Charles States Andrew, lived nearby. Richard's other three brothers, Fred, Nathaniel, and Robert, returned to Boston frequently and considered it to be their home.

Andrew settled at 15 Tremont Street in Boston, taking commissions for portraits and landscapes. Besides exhibiting his art in various venues in Boston, Andrew exhibited some of his early works at the Pennsylvania Academy of Fine Arts. His painting entitled, "The Portrait," a watercolor, was shown there in 1896.

Andrew joined the Guild of Boston Artists, created at the turn of the twentieth century by Edmund Tarbell, Frank Weston Benson, Lilla Cabot Perry, and forty-two of Boston's leading painters. The primary purpose of the Guild was to enable these painters and sculptors to maintain a gallery of their own where they could exhibit their work. Membership there required one essential qualification: the professional competence of an artist in his or her field. To be a member of the Guild of Boston Artists, an organization that remains today, a painter or sculptor must know his trade. There is an intense preoccupation with workmanship, with those qualities of observation, rendering, and execution that are the principal elements of a painter's art. Andrew enjoyed this association and remained a member for many years.

He also joined the Gloucester Society of Artists. This was an unjuried rival of the North Shore Arts Association and the Rockport Art Association. The Gloucester Society of Artists began in July 1923, located at 59 Eastern Point Road. In 1948, it merged with the Rockport Artists Society to become the Cape Ann Society of Artists. That organization folded in the 1950s.

Little is known of Richard Andrew's social life. He was respected and loved by his many friends, relatives, and admirers, but whether or not he was a part of "the social set" is not known. Richard married Lucy Choate Pew, on September 12, 1905. He was thirty-six and Lucy was twenty-eight. It was the first and only marriage for both. The ceremony was performed by Reverend Rufus P. Hibbard in a church in Gloucester, Massachusetts.

Lucy was born on November 18, 1876, and was the youngest of three children. Both of her parents were born in Massachusetts and lived in Gloucester all of their lives. Her father was a fish merchant. In 1849, he established the John Pew & Son Fishing Company located on Main Street in Gloucester, Massachusetts. On March 31, 1906, a year after Richard and Lucy were married, "The biggest news to hit Gloucester—much less the fishing industry—was announced. Slade Gorton & Company, John Pew & Son, David B. Smith & Company would combine to form the Gorton -Pew Fisheries Company," according to the Gortons of Gloucester website. "Gloucester had already firmly established itself as the largest fish-producing port in the United States and second in the world. Instantly, the new company had a fleet of thirty-nine vessels, the largest fleet of any company on the Atlantic Coast."

These were exciting years for the Andrews as they watched the growth of the Gorton-Pew fishing company. Lucy's father was a proud and happy man, and he shared his success with his family.

The Andrews were summer residents of Wolf Hill, Gloucester, from 1913 until retiring in 1937. For their retirement, Andrew built and designed a Cape Cod home at 19 Grapevine Road in Gloucester. The house included a large studio, a small studio, and a gallery, that Andrew opened to the public in his later years. Kathi and Jim Turner own this home and proudly display Richard Andrew's blueprints for the home on their kitchen wall. They have renovated the studio to keep pace with the space needs of their three beautiful children, but have kept the charming original home intact.

The years Andrew lived in Gloucester, where shipbuilding and fishing industries thrived, gave him the tools to paint seascapes, ships, and boats with accuracy, respect, and beauty. Jen Fahey, a current resident of Grapevine Road, expressed the

following: "I should tell you that I'm rather delighted and quite interested to learn of another esteemed painter, Mr. Andrew, on 'Artists Row.' It is clear the muses were here, which is in no small way part of the happiness my husband and I feel living here!"

Lucy is known to have been fluent in French and was well educated. Her niece, Karen Kimball, stated, "I even have some of her books written in French in my possession still, up in the attic." Lucy's family was related to the Choate family, one of the original families to settle in Gloucester, Massachusetts.

From the portraits that Richard Andrew painted of her, Lucy was strikingly beautiful in an aristocratic way. It is also known from her letters that she was very close to Richard's family and that she excelled in her ability to cook and to do needlework. "She made the best fish chowder—really the best I ever had," stated her niece, Karen Kimball. She added, "Aunt Lucy and Uncle Dick had a very long marriage, at times challenging when stress was high, such as when there was a commission to finish. They were devoted to each other's needs and happiness."

They did not have any children. Lucy lived for several years after Andrew's death on July 12, 1956, and stayed in their Gloucester home on Grapevine Road for a year or so after he died. She later moved into town and died in February 1968.

Subject: Lucy Andrew
Oil on Canvas
10 x 13.5 in.
Private Collection, New Hampshire

Shipbuilding, Gloucester
Etching with Gouache
8.5 x 10 in.
Private Collection, New Hampshire

CAREER AS AN ART INSTRUCTOR
MASSACHUSETTS NORMAL SCHOOL OF ART

Richard Andrew
Yearbook Photo, 1927
Massachusetts Normal School
MassArt Archives

The Massachusetts Normal School, later to be known as MassArt, is a distinguished educational institution. The first art college in America, it was founded in 1873, with the purpose of satisfying two imperatives—a business demand for industrial drawing skills and the belief of educators that training in drawing could promulgate both manual and intellectual skills, and even yield spiritual benefits. The goal would be to educate people in the creative process, not merely train them to draw.

On October 1, 1901, Richard Andrew accepted a post as an instructor at his alma mater, Massachusetts Normal School of Art, where he later became Head of the Department of Graphic Art.

At first he taught drawing but soon he was made an instructor of upper level courses for those who were interested in becoming artists themselves. These courses included anatomy and drawing with specializations in etching and painting. Most years his students made comments about him in their yearbooks. These records reflect that Richard Andrew's character, strong personality, exceptional ability to draw anything, and to explain art and techniques clearly made him a favorite and well-respected teacher.

From the 1921 Annual Yearbook:

Richard Andrew. Instructor in charge of Graphic Art Department. "A man who lived up to his name, an' drew, an' drew, an' drew."

From the 1924 Annual Yearbook:

"Dry as a bone" is a phrase which does not apply to Mr. Andrew's anatomy class, even though it does include the study of bones! In fact, we cannot imagine any subject being uninteresting if it is taught by him, embellished by his humorous remarks and made comprehensible by his clear explanations. The human figure is not the only phase of art with which he is familiar, as is shown in the Boston Art Galleries where we find his landscapes in oil exhibited. "One of the finest life and anatomy instructors in the country," that is what is said of him by those who know, and we do not find it hard to believe them.

And from the 1925 Annual Yearbook:

Mr. Andrew is the exponent of free expression, the analyst of human beings, the teacher who injects vivid comments and dissertations into an ordinarily dull anatomy course, who secures amazingly faithful attendances to life classes and who kindly and sincerely helps us grow. But beware of the twinkle in his eyes! It precludes an argument, for Mr. Andrew talks of many things. Not only is Mr. Andrew a successful teacher but as well, a fine artist, as many Boston Art gallery exhibitions can prove.

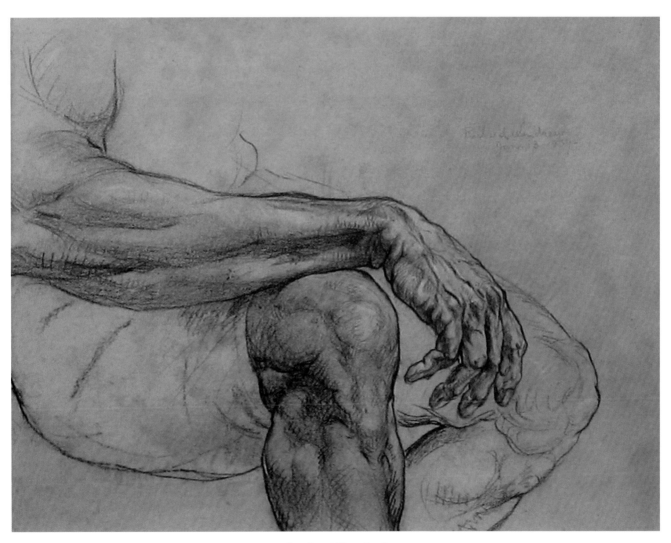

Hand and Knee Study
Graphite on Paper
9 x 8 in., 1939
Private Collection, Norwich, Vermont

From the 1930 Annual Yearbook:

We have only to talk with Mr. Andrew for five minutes and our education has increased immeasurably. Mr. Andrew is not only a well of knowledge of anatomy, but we defy anyone to name anything about which he doesn't know at least something. His intimate and informal lectures on anatomy are as interesting and delightful as the man himself; for who could dream that lessons on dull bones and muscles, and their wearying functions could be so permeated with a man's personality that they become vitally interesting and essential to every phase of art.

It was his lifelong experience as a recognized "teacher of art, muralist, painter/ artist, printmaker/graphic artist, which sharpened his intellect and abilities as he shared with his students the very essence of art.

Teaching was his career, coupled with his growing private art studio audience in quest of his murals, portraits, landscapes, seascapes, and shipbuilding paintings. The many exhibitions throughout the country and abroad where he showed his paintings made for a very busy and fruitful life.

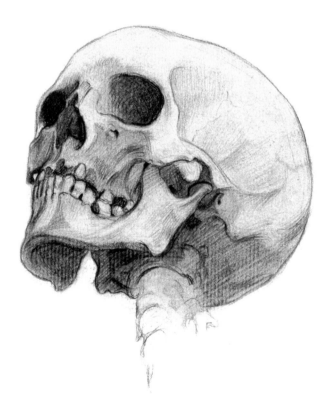

Skull
Graphite on Paper
6 x 7 in.
Private Collection,
Derbyshire, Vermont

A NOTE ON THE PORTRAIT BY RAYMOND A. PORTER
(A COLLEAGUE AT MASSACHUSETTS NORMAL SCHOOL)

Raymond Averill Porter and His Mother
1928 Annual Portfolio of Students of Massachusetts Normal School
Courtesy of MassArt Archives

Mr. Andrew's portrait of my mother and me was started about six years ago and although practically finished, it has not been finished to the satisfaction of the artist until now. The sittings were usually at my home, and Mother is shown in her accustomed chair with a silk log cabin quilt, one of a long series that she loved to build. They make a sort of tapestry of family vanities, and filled for her the place of more elaborate needlework too minute for old eyes.

If you find in this canvas delicate refinements of design and felicitous harmonies of tone, I assure you they are not accidental, nor can you credit them to the natural beauty of at least one of the sitters. The camera has always failed to achieve such results when used upon him. And if you find that your favorite theory of Art is applicable I can testify that it was applied if at all only after it had been demonstrated. The painter relied on his instinct and not on his book.

An artist such as Mr. Andrew at work is as alive and earnest as Vesuvius. If brushes with white lead or arsenic on them need to be pointed, no fear of poisoning stops their being pointed, and in the most natural way. If an afternoon's work is beautiful in its own way but not quite true in its own psychological balance, out it goes and another day of energetic attack gets the right balance.

These intermittent visits of Mr. Andrew to carry on the portrait when in the mood have been the occasion of many delightful discussion of art in all its phases; and now with the finished work before me, I personally feel greatly honored and deeply grateful.

HIS STUDENTS

N.C. WYETH

N.C. Wyeth
Courtesy of Brandywine Museum,
Chadds Ford, Pennsylvania
and Betsy Wyeth

In David Michaels' book, *N.C. Wyeth: A Biography*, he states that "During Andrew's first year as a teacher, 1901, N.C. Wyeth (Noel Convers Wyeth) enrolled in Richard Andrew's class. In Boston that fall, Convers Wyeth could not have been further from the action. Every morning Convers trudged into the Massachusetts Normal Art School in Boston. In drab classrooms, he listened as lecturers tried to arouse in the minds of the despairing pupils an interest in combined angles, shadow planes, vanishing points, foreshortened circles, roofing timbers, and other hopeless mysteries."

"The place lacked everything Convers felt his training should have. He wanted ecstasy. He wanted rigor. The boy wanted to be intoxicated by art. He longed for the days when 'an air of great seriousness, of religious fervor, surrounded the training of an artist.' In its small-town way, the Normal Art School tried to become the 'Paris of America.' But Convers found no light in his classes, no 'steadying influences of an intellectual nature.' Among the faculty no one to remind him that art and life are incorporate, that to grow in artistic power he must grow in character."

"All was not lost; Richard Andrew had studied in Paris, exhibited in Boston and began teaching in the school that same year. Opinionated, direct, forceful, Andrew educated his students not just in anatomy and life drawing, but also in the eclectic enthusiasms of an individualist. A burly Irishman, he kept students off-balance with caustic observations. When he evaluated Convers Wyeth's drawing of a fox's head, Andrew said that the work 'had the qualities of a drawing made for illustration.' Andrew suggested that Wyeth had the talent to become an illustrator and right there, Wyeth later remembered, 'I jumped at a straw.'"

It is well known that N.C. Wyeth went on to study illustration. He became one of America's most celebrated illustrators. It seems significant that by 1921, N.C. Wyeth could have sent his daughter anywhere in the world to study art, but chose to send Henrietta Wyeth to Massachusetts Normal Art School. There she studied Life Drawing under N.C. Wyeth's influential teacher, Richard Andrew.

Other students of Richard Andrew include:

MARGARET FITZHUGH BROWNE

Born in 1884, she was active in the art world not only as a painter, but also as a teacher, lecturer, writer, and critic. Her other noted teachers were Joseph DeCamp and Albert H. Munsell. She also studied at the Museum of Fine Arts in Boston, under Frank Weston Benson. While she did her studies there, she also took private lessons from Richard Andrew.

FREDERICK RYAN

He came from Prince Edward Island, Canada, in 1907. He studied with Richard Andrew and Ernest L. Major. Ryan exhibited his work in Paris at the Paris Salon in 1930: The Copley Society in Boston; The Providence Art Club; and many others.

CORA MILLET HOLDEN

She studied Decorative Figure Drawing with Richard Andrew. She became very widely acclaimed. Because she was competent in portrait painting, book illustration, sculpting, poster decorating, and mural painting, Georgie Norton, the director of the Cleveland School of Art, considered Holden something of a "phenomenon."

CHARLES RICHERT

As a professional, he later became a member of the Boston Water Color Society and the Boston Painter's Guild and exhibited widely.

MAURICE FREEDMAN   Freedman went on to study in Europe and became known for colorful oil landscapes, cityscapes, and seascapes using cubism and expressionism.

ANTON KAMP   He became a good friend of Richard Andrew's and served as a model for the Hall of Valor paintings in the Massachusetts State House. Kamp was also a student of and model for John Singer Sargent.

Photograph: *Richard Andrew and Anton Kamp*
1931 State House Murals
Private Collection, Boston, Massachusetts

THE ARTIST

Richard was the pride of the Andrew family, who followed every step of his career and accomplishments with joy and interest. Newly married and content in his personal life, Richard Andrew's career blossomed. His life began to change in other ways.

His brother, Robert, married Viola Ackeroyd, a violinist and seamstress from Boston. His brother, Buster, married Edwina Dobbins from Roxbury, Massachusetts. Their children became frequent models for Andrew's portraits, which were shown throughout the United States and abroad. Andrew and his wife, Lucy, were devoted to their nieces and stayed in constant touch with each of them throughout their lives. There were only four children in the next generation.

One of his early portraits was of his niece, Marguerite, in 1902, when she was a baby about six months old. The portrait is a head study of her with a soft blue wool bonnet tied gently below her chin.

Baby: Marguerite Andrew
Oil on Board
11.5 x 12.5 in., 1902
Private Collection,
Homestead, Florida

Andrew's reputation grew as commissions for his paintings reached new heights. Among many others, he painted four very large panels for the highly successful financier, Thomas W. Larson, to grace his mansion, "Greenwold," in Scituate, Massachusetts. He painted a portrait of Mr. Sherburne, headmaster of Jefferson School, for his Endicott home, as well as a portrait of Mr. Raymond A. Porter and his mother. Mr. Porter was a colleague of Andrew's at the Massachusetts Normal School of Art. (See page 39.) "The Violinist" was a portrait of the renowned musician, John Craig Kelley, and was exhibited in Chicago, Cincinnati, Boston, and Washington. These years were productive and rewarding for Richard Andrew and established him as an artist of record. He lived and worked in several locations in Boston and Ipswich. Among the addresses were 15 Tremont Street in 1896, 192 Boylston Street in 1906, 400 Northampton Street in 1907, Watson Street in 1908, and the Fenway Studios in 1926.

The following is a partial list of exhibitions and paintings by Richard Andrew:

Albright Art Gallery

Art Institute of Chicago
1906	The Violinist: *John Craig Kelley*
	Portrait of a Football Player
1907	Portrait of Miss B. and her dog, Teddy
	Portrait of Miss A.
1908	Portrait of Miss A.
1911	Autumn
1923	Girl with Blueberries
1924	Girl in Black Hat

Boston Art Club
1890	Strive for Masteries
1986	Glimpse of South Front Charles
	Portrait of Myself
1906	Still Life, Wild Swan
	On the Charles
	Portrait of Miss B.
1907	Portraits of a Mother and Daughter
1908	Cornelia

Boston City Club
1915	Spring – a decorative mural

Cincinnati Art Museum
1908	*Fifteenth Annual Exhibition of American Art, held from May 23 to July 20*
	The Violinist

Copley Gallery, 103 Newbury St. Boston
1941	Autumn
	The Violinist
	Portrait of Girl in Black
	Mrs. A
	Portrait of Girl in Yellow
	The Golden Rose
	Interior – The Quiet Afternoon
	Richard Andrew
	Summer Evening – Decoration
	Scudding Clouds
	My Father
	Mid-Summer
	After-Glow
	Mrs. A
	Marine – The Pink Rocks
	Portrait of a Young Man
	Winter Sunset
	Spring
	Salt Barque, Gloucester Harbor
	The Cabbage Field
	Crowned with Fire

Corcoran Gallery, Washington, DC
1907　The Violinist
1912　Autumn

Cornell University Four Man Exhibition
1908　Several Portraits
　　　The Football Player
　　　Portrait of Lucy Pew Andrew

Exhibition of American Art, Poland Spring, Maine
1908　Canoeing

Guild of Boston Artists
1918　Portrait Group
　　　Portrait Miss Edna Tremains
　　　Portrait Arthur Dallin (French Army)
　　　Lady in Black Furs
　　　Portrait Mrs. Frank C. Parmenter
　　　Girl Scout
　　　The School Girl
　　　Sewing for Belgian Babies
　　　Portrait of a Man
　　　Portrait Mr. Vesper L. George (Illustrator)
　　　The Blueberry Girl
　　　Portrait Sergt. Frederick Elwood Wallace
　　　Portrait of a Lady
　　　Portrait Mr. Henry O'Connor (Artist)
　　　Portrait Mr. Derrick C. Parmenter
　　　Portrait Mr. J.C.S. Andrew

1919　Professor J.C.S. Andrew (Army Education Corps)
　　　John Crossman (artillery)
　　　Ensign C.E.B. Navy
　　　Egg Rock
　　　My Father
　　　Sun Sparkles
　　　Surf Rings
　　　The Big Maple
　　　Esparanto off Grapevine Cove
　　　The Old Barn
　　　Cape Ann Rocks
　　　Decorative Landscape
　　　King's Beach
　　　The Freshening Breeze
　　　Braces Rock by Moonlight
　　　Off Nahant
　　　Unsettled Weather

Whistler House Museum, Lowell, Massachusetts
1940's to present
　　　Self-portrait 1934
　　　Thatcher Light
　　　Sunlit Rocks

The MacDowell Club of New York, 108 West 55th St., New York City
1912　Girl in Black
　　　Autumn
　　　Quiet Afternoon

Museum of Fine Arts Boston
(John Singer Sargent and Edmund Tarbell also showed in this exhibition)
1920　Portrait

Panama-Pacific International Exposition, San Francisco
1916　By the River

Pennsylvania Academy of Fine Arts
1896-97 Portrait
1905　Portrait of J.C.S. Andrew
1906　Portrait of a Football Player
1907　Portrait of Mrs. A
　　　Portrait of Miss B and Her Dog Teddy
1908　Violinist
1909　Portrait of My Father
1911　Autumn
1914　Summer Afternoon
1918　Portrait: Arthur Dallin
　　　(Dallin was a stained glass artist)
1919　Surf Rings
　　　The Schoolgirl
1920　Portrait: John Crossman
　　　Portrait: Professor J.G.S. Andrew
1934　Self-Portrait

This list is not necessarily complete. There is evidence that Richard Andrew also exhibited in Europe.

AT WORK IN HIS COMMUNITY

The Museum of Fine Arts in Boston occasionally featured Richard Andrew as a guest lecturer for their "Fine Arts Talk." On May 14, 1911, he spoke on the topic "Likeness in Painting." A lecture on December 18, 1914, was entitled "Why an Artist's Style Changes." As his students reported in yearbook after yearbook, Richard Andrew was a respected and entertaining speaker.

Andrew was a popular Boston artist, and he generously contributed his talents to a variety of projects throughout the city. On February 17, 1915, *The Boston Daily Globe* printed a headline that read "BOSTON CITY CLUB'S NEW HOME: $900,000 Building at the Corner of Ashburton Place Will Be Opened for Use Feb. 15." The article, under the heading "Art Treasures," read, "A number of valuable oil paintings adorn the walls. There are five pieces by Philip Little, copies of Valasquez, favorite of the Art Museum and one entitled, 'Spring' by Richard Andrew of the Normal Art School." This very large mural is a companion piece to "Autumn." "Autumn" was painted for the City Club of Boston. It is now owned by Furman University in Greenville, South Carolina. There were also four season-themed panels designed for Thomas W. Lawson, one of the most successful businessmen in Boston at the time. (See Section III, Page 141.)

A reflection on the state of the war in 1915, the *Boston Daily Globe* published the article "WAR POSTERS BRING HOME TO PATRIOTS NECESSITY OF BUYING LIBERTY BONDS." The article noted that "the poster, 'Our National Ideals' by Arthur Spear, is another dramatic comment on culture, as is 'A Just Peace' by Richard Andrew."

On March 10, 1918, *The Boston Globe* featured an article, "POSTERS FOR FLOWER SHOW: More Than Fifty Artists Have Drawn Them for the Benefit of the Red Cross Exhibition." It read, "One of the best collections ever designed for a show for entertainment in this city has been done for the Red Cross Flower Show to be held in the Horticultural Hall from the 13th to the 17th of March." Richard Andrew was listed as one of those contributors.

At The Alexandra, Boston
Watercolor on Paper
17.5 x 13.5 in., c.1890
Private Collection, Derbyshire, Vermont

An exemplary and dedicated teacher, Richard Andrew was pleased to accept the opportunity to supervise students in a very challenging artistic endeavor. *The Boston Globe*, June 19, 1927, featured an article, "Unveil Pictures by Boston Art Students," that hailed the work of Richard Andrew's students at the Bridgewater Normal School for the murals in the new auditorium. It stated:

> "Contrary to the views of several, Richard Andrew assured the committee that seniors in the art class were perfectly capable of painting six murals 5.5 feet by 11.5 feet each to celebrate the opening of the school's new auditorium. Mr. Andrew in speaking of the work said: *'They have exceeded my expectations and I am very gratified that the students have been able to carry it out in the manner that they did. It is an achievement that the institution may well be proud of.'*"

As a teacher par excellence, he applied discipline and affection in equal measures to assist his students in achieving their very best. As of spring 2009, the college completed renovations of the auditorium highlighting these classic works of art that depict the history of education.

"A Trained Teacher for Every Child" and *"The Truth Shall Make You Free"*
Selected murals of the Horace Mann Auditorium
Bridgewater State College, Bridegewater, Massachusetts

The height of Richard Andrew's career is a fascinating account. In 1924 at the age of fifty-five, he won the competition sponsored by the Massachusetts State House and the Massachusetts Art Commission to paint the Hall of Valor to decorate the third floor of the State House. (See Part II.) **He painted an astonishing wealth of portraits,** studies and sketches, landscapes **and seascapes, more examples of which will be featured in Part III.**

19 Grape Vine Road
Eastern Point
Gloucester Massachusetts

Sept. 2 - 1937.

Mr C. Edward Newell,
Mass. School of Art,

My dear Mr. Newell,

Having served long and faithfully as an instructor in the Massachusetts School of Art I now request that my resignation be accepted.

Respectfully
Richard Andrew.

Self-portrait
Graphite on Paper
6 x 8.5 in.
Private Collection, Boston, Massachusetts

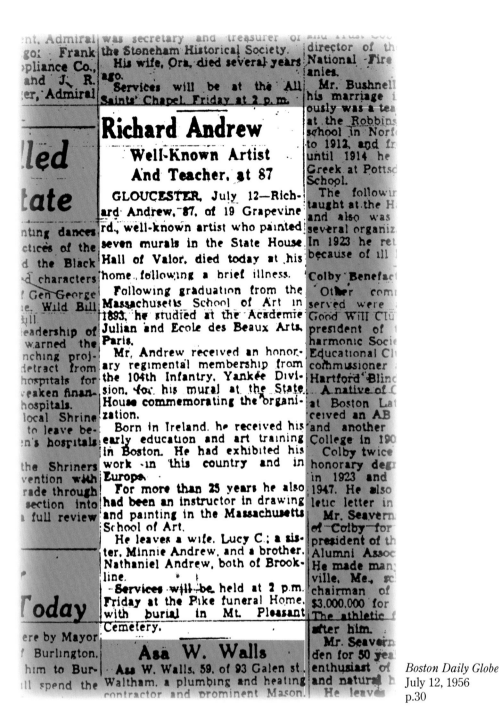

Boston Daily Globe
July 12, 1956
p.30

Richard Andrew passed away in his home at 19 Grapevine Road in Gloucester, Massachusetts, on July 12, 1956. He was eighty-seven years old. The title of his obituary from *The Boston Globe* was titled: "Richard Andrew, Well-Known Artist and Teacher." It stated, "He received an honorary membership from the 104th Infantry, Yankee Division, for his murals at the Massachusetts State House commemorating their courage and history."

To reflect upon the person who was Richard Andrew those people who knew him well, often said, "Whenever Richard Andrew was mentioned, there was quick attention and hushed reverence." He was extremely intelligent, very well educated, and he could talk on almost any subject with clarity and conviction. His sense of humor made him dear to his students, family, and friends.

Donagal Headlands
Guild of Boston Artists
Exhibition: May 1-23, 1942
Oil on Board
36 x 48 in.
Private Collection, Boston, Massachusetts

Though proud of his Scottish heritage, he made repeated trips to his beloved Ireland throughout his life, and painted some of his brightest and most colorful landscapes there. Like his parents, he enjoyed traveling abroad.

A very focused and intense man, Richard Andrew cared deeply about his art and his teaching. The students he taught remember him with praise and a smile. His quick sense of humor and broad scope of knowledge on virtually any subject made him an "awe inspiring instructor."

Formidable in his critiques and expectations, he was beloved and respected. He did not tolerate interference in his creative process. Relatives and friends knew better than to ask to see him when he was painting, so intense was he. His wife, Lucy, guarded his privacy with care.

At maturity, Richard Andrew was the picture of a Scottish gentleman, five feet nine inches tall and squarely built. His bushy eyebrows, twinkling blue eyes, ready smile, and commanding presence made him the center of attention. Raised in genteel circumstances, Richard wore a shirt and tie, even when painting. He was every bit a gentleman.

Richard Andrew's talents have lived on these many years since his death in 1956. Appreciation of his works is higher now than ever. Love of the man will continue, as evidenced by those who own his paintings and have so kindly and enthusiastically endorsed this book. He left us the riches of his personal life of kindness and loyalty, and his extraordinary talents are recognized still from all around this country and abroad.

Richard Andrew
Photo by Anton Kamp
Private Collection, Kensington, New Hampshire

Edwina Andrew Portraits

The Flapper

Page 16

Nicknamed, "The Duchess," because of her likeness to the Prince of Wales' consort, "the Duchess of Windsor." Edwina Andrew, born in 1909, lived during a period when fashion, style, and high living ruled the day. These were the years when Rockefeller, Goodyear, Crane, and others, had parties to remember. The industrial giants set the tone, and being part of it determined one's status in society.

Until the ninth grade, Edwina lived in Yellville, Arkansas; Cripple Creek, Colorado; and Joplin, Missouri, where her father and Uncle Bob owned and operated silver and lead mines. They moved to Boston, where she attended the Choate School and graduated from Wheelock College. She was a debutante whose "coming out" party was held at Longwood Towers in Boston, Massachusetts.

Edwina was so attractive and, in fact, beautiful, that her popularity was assured. Throughout her life, she was a delight to everyone who knew her. The joyful way she faced life made her unforgettable to her friends and family.

Edwina was the model for the portrait "The Flapper," wearing a white feather hat and Chinese wrap.

Girl with a Lantern

Page 100

Andrew painted "Girl with a Lantern" in 1917. One afternoon, Edwina, an eight-year old, was playing in her Uncle Dick's studio in Gloucester, Massachusetts. She picked up an orange lantern and looked into it.

Her Uncle Dick glanced over at this enchanting child and saw the potential for an oil painting of his great niece, daughter of his brother Buster. Adored by her uncle, Richard Andrew, this is one of the many paintings he made of her.

Uncle Dick, as Edwina called him, so enjoyed this little girl that he hand made a tea set complete with a little wooden table and chairs for her to play with.

PART II: HALL OF VALOR
"TIN HELMETS AND CLAY FIGURES"

RICHARD ANDREW AND THE MASSACHUSETTS STATE HOUSE MURALS

"The picture itself is a marvel. And it may well cause the schools of Boston—to sit up and take notice. This city imported Sargent and Abbey to decorate the public buildings not only because their works were beautiful, but because they were strong. And here is a Boston man about to take his place beside the others, earning that position by the rugged truth, the artistic quality, and that powerful interpretation of his canvas."

–Frederick O'Hara, January 16, 1927, *The Boston Globe.*

Mural Study
Charcoal and Chalk on Paper
15.5 x 20 in., c. 1927
Private Collection, Kensington, New Hampshire

INTRODUCTION: HISTORICAL SETTING

It is interesting to put into perspective the years of Richard Andrew's life from the late 1880s to 1917. A period of confidence and tranquility, no one dreamt of the chaos to come when the United States would enter World War I.

The creativity of man seemed endless, even as it does today. Alexander Graham Bell's invention of the telephone in 1876 revolutionized communication. Ocean liners sped across the sea drawing people and nations closer. Thomas Edison began marketing electric lighting by 1882. Basic to home and business, it eliminated the arduous task of cleaning and filling kerosene lamps. Life's pace quickened with inventions using electricity.

In 1870, the year after Richard Andrew's birth, the Transcontinental Railroad opened. John D. Rockefeller Jr., a business titan, provided enormous opportunities worldwide by creating oil and railroad dynasties. The charitable foundations he created gave impetus to scientific, educational, and medical advances. The stock market flourished. In 1886, the Statue of Liberty, a gift from France as a symbol of national friendship and liberty, was dedicated.

American art was blessed by Winslow Homer's great artworks observing mankind. John Singer Sargent contributed his talents in portraiture, landscapes, and murals. The Hudson River School of Art, renowned for its beautiful landscapes, dominated the American art world.

In 1908, Henry Ford invented the Model T automobile that was to profoundly change the world. Mark Twain, Leo Tolstoy, F. Scott Fitzgerald, Jack London, and many other authors delighted the public with their writing. The Wright brothers flew the world's first airplane in Kitty Hawk, North Carolina. Radio and motion pictures became new pleasures and contributed to the excitement of this period of growth.

All of these developments and more were happening at the time Richard Andrew was becoming one of Boston's fine American artists, with the height of his career yet to come.

WORLD WAR I: THE 104TH INFANTRY

World War I shocked the United States with its savagery, boldness, and the surprising success of the German Army's aggression toward European nations. Slow to join the conflict, the United States declared war in 1917 and sent troops, including the Massachusetts 104th Infantry, to fight alongside the Allies.

ONE HUNDREDTH AND FOURTH INFANTRY:
A RECOUNT OF THE BATTLE THAT TURNED THE COURSE OF THE FIRST WORLD WAR

Boston Evening Transcript
April 5, 1924

On the morning of April 10, 1918, following an hour of bombardment, the Germans attacked the lines held by the 104th, upwards of 800 shock troops, being used. The Americans had been holding the spot, before the German-occupied town of Apremont, for several days when this attack was made and it was evident that the Germans had learned the identity of the troops facing them and had determined to strike a crushing blow for the effect it would have on the morale of the Americans.

On April 10th, 12th and 13th, suffering from very heavy bombardments and attacked by very strong German forces, the One Hundred and Fourth Infantry succeeded in preventing their dangerous advance, and with greatest energy re-conquered, at the point of bayonet, the few ruined trenches which had to be abandoned at the first onset, at the same time taking prisoners.

On May 3, 1918, the following story of the decoration of the colors by General Passaga appeared in the 'Stars and Stripes:' On a high plateau within a few kilometers of the German lines, with the sun just smiling through the mist like a mother through her proud tears, a French army corps commander decorated 117 members

Soldier Study
Charcoal and Chalk on Paper
20.5 x 6.25 in., c.1927
Private Collection, Kensington, NH

of the One Hundred and Fourth Infantry, Massachusetts, with the Croix de Guerre on Sunday afternoon, April 28, 1917. The regimental colors of the One Hundredth and Fourth also were decorated.

The One Hundred and Fourth Infantry is the First American regiment in any war to be so honored. The award was made for the signal bravery the regiment showed in the three day fight in and about Apremont Wood, which began April 10, and during which a bitter onslaught of the Germans was repulsed with great enemy losses. The regiment, heavily bombarded and attacked by superior numbers, checked the Huns' advances and retook the trench from which it had fallen back, capturing numerous prisoners in its brave stand.

How Decoration Was Given

Except for the sound of the German guns reverberating through the lowlands, the plateau where the decorations were made might almost have been Boston Common. The men were the same kind of men who, one April day, one hundred and forty years ago, at Lexington and Concord fought for the same ideals of world honor and democracy.

As the regiment arrived at the reviewing ground, it was formed in line and prepared to pass in review. At the reviewing stand were the regimental colors and the soldiers who had been decorated. These faced the regiment, and stood about six paces in the rear of the reviewing officers. Led by the regimental band, the entire regiment, in column of companies, passed in review.

And as the regiment, sturdy and upstanding, marched by their commanding general and the French commander, it was an effort for the onlooker to restrain a cheer; it was impossible, by any effort, to keep the lump out of the throat; and the eyes of many French and Americans watching the inspiring sight cloud up with pardonable tears.

It was another of those times when you felt like turning a somersault with pride, just because you were an American. And as the American general went up to each of the honored men, giving him a personal and friendly word of appreciation and congratulation, every man in the regiment and every other man who witnessed it knew that the general was the spokesman of the whole United States, here and at home. The Nation, great and grateful, was thanking, through the general, these men for their part in keeping it great.

As the regimental band played the first bars of "The Star Spangled Banner," and merged in 'La Marseillaise,' the French general, expressing his pride at decorating the colors of a regiment that had shown such bravery, walked to the regimental colors and tied to the top of the staff the red and green ribbon, the bronze Croix de Guerre hanging therefrom. Then the general decorated the regiment's commander, Colonel George H. Shelton, and 116 officers and men of the 104th.

This is the story that foretells the decision of the Massachusetts Legislature and the Massachusetts Art Commission to decorate the walls on the third floor Legislative Chambers' halls. With pride in the glory of its 104th Infantry action on April 18, 1918, a commission was formed to select an artist to design and paint murals to celebrate and commemorate this most important group of brave men from Massachusetts who changed the course of World War I.

Photograph: *One Hundred and Fourth Infantry*
Third Floor, Massachusetts State House, Boston

MASSACHUSETTS LEGISLATIVE RESOLUTIONS

The inspiration to honor the members of the 104th Regiment Infantry commenced in 1922. A special commission was formed by the Legislature and authorized by the Governor to create a competition to find the best artist to paint the murals as determined by legislative resolves. The Legislative Commission should act jointly with the Art Commission. The Art Commission is to be composed of members of the Senate, appointed by the President of the Senate, and two members of the House, appointed by the Speaker, as well as three persons appointed by the governor.

The Resolves of the Commonwealth of Massachusetts

"An Act Authorizing the Placing in the State House of a Memorial in Honor of the One Hundred and Fourth Regiment Infantry who lost their lives in the World War." House Document No.1280, 1922. x 496, 1924 on petition of Merle D. Graves.

"Resolve to provide for the Suitable Commemoration of the decoration by the French Republic during the World War of the Colors of the One Hundred and Fourth Infantry of the Twenty-Sixth Division."
House Document No. 496, 1924.

"Resolve to provide for the Suitable Commemoration of the Decoration by the French Republic during the World War of the Colors of the One Hundred and Fourth Infantry of the Twenty-Sixth Division." Resolves of 1924, Chapter 19.

Resolved: that in testimony of the commonwealth's appreciation of the services rendered by the men from Massachusetts who served in the World War and to commemorate the signal honor to those men and to the commonwealth as evidenced by the decoration by the French Republic, during the World War of the colors of the 104th Infantry of the twenty-sixth division, which regiment was the first unit of American troops to be so honored by a foreign government during the history of our nation, and to properly impress our citizens of this and future generations with the importance of such honor, it is hereby directed that a fitting mural decoration, representing such event, be placed in the state house. For this purpose, such sum not exceeding $8,000, (equals $91,000 in 2006), as may hereafter be appropriated may be expended by a commission appointed by the governor, who shall, together with the art commission of the commonwealth arrange therefore and who shall, subject to the approval of said art commission, select a site within the state house for such mural decoration. Approved April 15, 1924.

The Yankee Division Commission was appointed on June 26, 1924 and composed of:

General Alfred F. Foote, Holyoke, State Director of Public Safety
Major Edward J. Connelly, Wakefield
Major Thomas J. Hammond, Northfield
Crawford J. Furguson, Brighton
Major Alfred F. Bailot, Adams
Sergeant Patrick J. Gloster, Springfield

Photograph: *Richard Andrew*
Private Collection, Boston, Massachusetts

Winning the Competition

Boston Sunday Globe
July 15, 1924 p.13

Richard Andrew, Boston, Wins Competition Scene Depicting the Decorating of the Colors of Noted Regiment to be Located on Third Floor of Building

Richard Andrew, a prominent Boston artist, was today awarded the contract to paint the new military portrait for the State House Commission created for that purpose. Under the terms of the act authorizing the painting it was stipulated that the work must be done by a resident of Massachusetts, or by a member of the twenty-sixth Division, and the joint commission in seeking the best artist available held a competition, offering three prizes for the best work submitted. As a result, Richard Andrew was awarded the commission. The second prize went to George Hallowell of Winchester, while two Yankee Division Veterans, J. Andrew Twachtman of Greenwich, Connecticut and Pelham Glassford of Washington, D.C. in collaboration won third prize.

The award-winning portrait will depict an incident of the World War which created military precedent—the decorating of the regimental colors of the 104th Infantry Yankee Division. This was more remarkable because it was the first time in the history of our country that any foreign power had ever decorated a unit of America's armed forces.

The picture is to be painted in three panels, nine feet in height and with a total length of twenty-six feet. This portrait will be placed on the third floor of the (Massachusetts) State House directly opposite the entrance to the House of Representatives, near the office of the secretary of state.

Every effort has been made to have the historical details of this painting accurate, and to this end many officers, and men of the division have been interviewed. It is the intention of the commission to have the picture completed and placed in position on April 27, 1927, the ninth anniversary of the actual decoration of the colors.

One Hundred and Fourth Infantry Division Mural
Oil on Canvas
111 x 192 in., 1927
Massachusetts State House, Boston

ABOUT THE MURAL

The 104th Infantry received the Croix de Guerre, with palm, for valiancy in the field, especially at Apremont—the first American troops to be so honored by a foreign government. Massachusetts unveiled a mural on April 30, 1927, to show her gratitude for services rendered by all her men in World War I, commemorating the signal honor of the 104th Regiment whose famous 26th (Yankee) Division was made up of New England men.

The painting is divided into three rectangular sections by two fluted pilasters. Upright allegorical panels fill each end, while the center horizontal space illustrates the scene at Boucq, France, that April day.

Richard Andrew painted the moment General Passaga tied the Croix de Guerre on the 104th regimental flag. The book, *The Massachusetts State House*, notes that Andrew said, "I am proud to decorate the flag of a nation which has come to our aid in the fight for liberty." Mr. Andrew's interpretation of color and action here is entirely realistic. (See photographs on page 70.)

Columbia and Gallia on each side, however, are symbolic. Columbia offers her sword to the aid of France, commemorating the 150 years of friendship. Gallia (the personification of France) supported by Joan of Arc (the patron saint of patriotism), reciprocates, awarding a wreath of honor to the men of the 104th Regiment.

The service flag is shown in memory of those heroes fallen in battle. Bronze coats of arms of France and Massachusetts completed this memorial. The flag that General Passaga decorated and the Croix de Guerre that he tied upon it are in Memorial Hall.

Detail of Mural showing Croix de Guerre

Artist Praises Herald's Reproduction in Colors of War Murals in Roto Today

The Boston Herald
Sunday Feb. 4, 1934. p.1, 22

Mr. Richard Andrew painted the murals at the North Shore galleries in Gloucester. He completed them in two years. The work is 9 feet in depth and 17 feet in length with smaller panels on either side.

Mr. Andrew explained that his purpose in painting the picture was to reveal the grim intent of the American troops as contrasted to the gallant attitude of the French officers.

Observe the faces of the Americans on the left of the painting, said Mr. Andrew. *They had just engaged in their first trying conflict and naturally were thoughtful of the reality of war. Knowing that they were in that frame of mind, I endeavored to convey the impression that they were but home-loving men who hated war, but were determined to end it and forget it.*

I tried to lend gallantry to the Frenchmen on the right because France had been at war so often that her soldiers thought it an avocation and looked upon war with nonchalance.

When beginning the picture, I resolved to paint it with strong heroic detail; yet not too melodramatic. I decided that if people were to be impressed with the magnificence of the Massachusetts division and with the horror of war, it would not do to execute a pale, lifeless mural with the aspect of a chocolate éclair crushed between two sidewalk bricks.

Detail of left panel

Of all the favorable comments received since painting the mural, I was most impressed by an elderly woman who approached me at the State House after the unveiling exercises. Although she had been crying, she spoke up bravely and said, "One of those gold stars on the left panel is for my son."

Mr. Andrew was born in Armagh, County Down, Ireland, and is the last descendent of the first Richard Andrew, who, as a child was found standing beside the body of his father who was killed when the Irish forces defeated the English warriors in the battle of Benberg in 1646.

A First Person Account
Tin Helmets and Clay Figures Inspire Great War Picture of Local Artist

Richard Andrew Finishing Memorial of 104th Regiment for the State House in His Fenway Studio – Photograph, Skeletons of Eagles, Imagination, and Living Models Combine to Recreate Famous Moment

Boston Sunday Globe
January 16, 1927
Editorial Section p.13
By Frederick O'Hara

Mr. Andrew's Design for State House Memorial to 104th Infantry Changes Made to This Design are Explained in the Story.

A monument to one of the glowing incidents in the history of American troops, and certainly the most brilliant in the record of the 104th Regiment of the Yankee Division, is fast materializing beneath the brush of Richard Andrew in his Fenway studio on Ipswich St.

For seven days in April, 1918, the 104th Regiment withstood continued bombardment and infantry attack, while holding the weakest point of the Allied line in the Apremont sector. On April 12, after seven days of battle, called upon by the adjoining hard-pressed French for a flanking movement, it engaged the Boche in hand- to-hand conflict and broke his attack.

On the afternoon of April 28, 1918, the regiment marched to Boucq, where General Passaga decorated the colors and the men of the regiment with the Croix de Guerre. It was the first time that a foreign power ever decorated the colors of an American regiment.

On April 28, 1927, the ninth anniversary, there will be unveiled in the State House a mural painting commemorating the event.

The work will be Mr. Andrew's, he having been chosen by the State Art Commission and the Yankee Division Committee.

The Type for Such a Picture

Behind the quaint brass knocker of a studio in the Fenway, the work is going on—a monumental task that will save for posterity a vivid picture of one of New England's greatest events. The artist, Andrew, is exactly the type to paint such a picture. Short but powerfully built, with a chest like a barrel, a square jaw, blue eyes twinkling beneath a shock of tousled grey hair, he is almost one of the soldiers that he paints, as he stumps about his studio in heavy army shoes.

The picture itself is a marvel. And it may well cause the schools of Boston—to sit up and take notice. This city imported Sargent and Abbey to decorate the public buildings, not only because their works were beautiful but also because they were strong. And here is a Boston man about to take his place beside the others, earning that position by the rugged truth, the artistic quality, and the powerful interpretation of his canvas.

Photograph: *Richard Andrew*
Private Collection, Boston, Massachusetts

Idea Given by Photograph

The idea for the central panel was supplied by an army photograph taken of the scene back in 1918. That was what the committee supplied to all the contestants for the commission. Of course, as you see, there is not much there other than the bare idea, but the artist was asked to incorporate that arrangement into his own composition.

As you see from the sketch the colors have been slanted—the commander salutes—the regiment presents arms, while General Passaga ties the medal upon the peak of the staff. In the panel beneath there will probably be inscribed the citation he made at the time. Andrew states, *I am proud to decorate the flag of a regiment which has such fortitude and courage; I am proud to decorate the flag of a nation which has come to our aid in the fight for liberty.*

General Edwards at Review at Boucq. France

To avoid the necessity of having printed explanations to pass out to all who might view the work, I decided upon the two side panels to offer explanation as well as to add classicism. On the left you see the figure of Columbia, supported by the American eagle, offering her sword to the aid of France. On the other side stands Gallia, the figure of the French Republic, supported by Jean D'Arc, the saint of patriotism, responding by offering a wreath of valor to the American troops.

Long Time on the Panels

Gosh, he went on, *I certainly spent a lot of time on those two panels. Three months I fussed and fumed—made arrangements and tore them up. Finally, so help me, I banged out the arrangements for the two panels inside of two hours. Funny, isn't it, how things work out sometimes?*

Placing Croix de Guerre on Regiment's Flag

Photographs:
Boston Evening Transcript
Mural Painting for State House to Commemorate
the Decoration of 104th Infantry
April 5, 1924, pt. 4, p. 3

"Seems to me," I ventured, "that I remember seeing some stories in the papers about your difficulty in securing models for the types."

Yes I did. But in Miss Marie Thomas of Auburndale of French parents, I found very much what I needed. She is 18 years old, the age of Jean D'Arc, at the time of her triumph. She is the ideal type with a sturdy figure and saintly expression; I used her for the head of Joan. For the figure – let me show you.

He led me into the adjoining room where he had a kneeling figure of a girl modeled in clay about a foot and a half high. About her he had fashioned miniature armor, painted with silver leaf, giving the glistening effect of polished steel.

This is what I used for the figure. He said simply. *It's a little damaged, for I have just moved everything up here from Gloucester.*

Started in July

I started the work in a studio down there. Let me see. It was about July when I commenced the final canvas and I worked steadily until about a week ago. I had previously gathered all the necessary material – sketches and so on.

He reached for a portfolio. It is amazing the amount of research work that the artist is demanded to make for such a problem.

Mural Study: Columbia
Charcoal on Paper
Private Collection, San Francisco, California

There was sketch after sketch of nude figures, figures kneeling, figures beginning to kneel, figures that appeared to be rising from a kneeling posture—all studies for the gesture and structure for Jean D'Arc. He pointed out where one drawing had something he could use. Another something else.

He had sketches and photographs of medieval armor, studies for the figure of Columbia, many varied poses. He had charcoal and chalk drawings of strong, rugged masculine types that would typify the fighting men. He had gone down to the Museum of Natural History and sketched eagles, dragging out the skeletons of eagles and making sketches of the bones, so that he could construct the bird in any position he desired. He had tin helmets and rifles in the corner. In fact, he had sketches of everything he needed for the accurate completion of every detail of the work.

Saw the Men Themselves

Some time ago, he said, *I went to Springfield, at the time of the reunion of the regiment, as the guest of General Foote, to get a line on the men What a fine lot of men they were! While there believe I really caught the spirit of the subject.*

Recently several of the men of the regiment came to the studio to see the work and exclaimed, 'Gosh—don't we look hard-boiled, though.' — making quite evident their satisfaction with the representation. It might be of interest to know that every man who posed for me had seen service overseas.

Everything wasn't smooth sailing even after that. He said, in answer to my question. *You will notice in the sketch that the top of the flag projects out of the picture. Well somebody else noticed it and for the sake of the safety all around, it was decided to lower the flag so that it would be all in the picture, the reason being sentimental and not military as far as I could make out. When I lowered the position of the flag I found it threw the men out of scale. So I had to redraw everything to go with the flag in its new relation. Not so good.*

And then again, it must be a portrait of General Passaga and all I have is this very poor print in which the figure is very small, giving little or no information as to what he actually looks like. The committee has sent to France in hopes of securing some good photographs of him.

Eagle Study
Chalk on Paper
12 x 7 in.
Private Collection, Norwich, Vermont

Mural Study
Oil on Board
20 x 14 in. c. 1927
Private Collection, Derbyshire, Vermont

How He Got Proportions

Yes, I use dynamic symmetry, but more as a checkup after I have composed my picture. Now, take this for example. I applied it in the laying out of the final canvas. I centered the national flag, drew an equilateral triangle, using the base of the canvas as the base of the triangle, and it decided the relative positions of Gen. Passaga and his aide with the saluting figure. A hexagon, centered on the canvas, determined the relative bulk of the four central figures, the cloud formation and the regimental colors. You see that it was necessary to make several slight changes from the original composition. But see how more compact the arrangement is than the original sketch. Also the light and shade can be determined by the same method. Great stuff for checking up, I find.

The trouble with this business—decoration, I mean – is that the architects were afraid of color in a building. They did not think they needed it. It is true that there has always been mural painting. But for the greater part it was done for Gothic architecture. In this country they have a different style of architecture. It is simpler, more like the classic Greek. The architects disliked great splashes of color and solid form. You can't blame them. It tore all their ideas to pieces. Brangwyn's things look fine, magnificent in Gothic rooms. But that attitude is not successful in this country.

The decoration can not be like the easel picture, in which the interest is centered. The mural painting must keep the interest all over the canvas, otherwise the wall will disappear and of course the architects will get peeved. I believe that this is my style of painting. I trained for decoration. That is my forte. I am not built to paint easel paintings. Like the architect, the decorator must deal with organized forms. If he starts running into atmosphere or third dimension he is on his game.

Hanging an Art in Itself

This picture must be placed April 1, so I shall start the last week in March to get it up. I might want to paint a bit on it after it is hung.

And hanging murals is an interesting task. The canvas must be taken from the stretcher and glued to the wall. In mounting, Venice turpentine is mixed with heavy white lead ground in oil, forming a heavy glue. It is put on the wall with a trowel while another bunch of men apply the glue to the canvas which is suspended from the ceiling by an iron bar running across the top.

It is allowed to set for about three hours, when it is centered and rolled out to all sides after the fashion of mounting a large photograph. Oftentimes the canvas will stretch as much as an inch in length and width. Then the painter must reconstruct certain resultant flaws along the edges. It takes about 6 months thoroughly to dry—then it is up to stay. Any attempt to pull it off results in a complete ruin of the picture.

"Did you ever run into serious difficulty?" I asked.

Yes, once. Some years ago I was commissioned by the late Thomas Lawson to paint the four seasons for his country home in Scituate. They were ceiling panels and the man engaged to hang the paintings evidently was not so good, for he had no sooner got them in place, when blooey—they all came tumbling down on the floor. You can imagine just about how mad I was. I gave the fellow one look and decided that I had better go out and have something to eat. When I returned you may be sure that he had beaten a hasty retreat. I had learned my lesson, and so immediately proceeded to learn the craft of mural painting hanging.

Mr. Andrew has exhibited in annual shows in this country and abroad. His works included decorations for the Endicott home, portraits of Mr. Sherburne, retired headmaster of the Jefferson School, Mr. Dutton and others.

Prop Sword
Private Collection, Shrewsbury, Massachusetts

Opposite:
Study: General Passaga and Gustav Gacon
Charcoal and Chalk on Paper
13 x 25 in., 1927
Private Collection, Orleans, Massachusetts

The French Captain and Columbia

Richard Andrew's life and legacy would not be complete without mention of the devotion and friendship he shared with Paul Adrian Brodeur. They met during the 1920s, when Andrew was an instructor at Massachusetts Normal School, and Brodeur, an orthodontist and bas-relief-sculptor, was his student. Over the next thirty years, the teacher-student relationship grew, and they remained close friends until the end of Andrew's life.

Upon winning the competition to paint the mural of the Massachusetts 104th Infantry Regiment, Andrew chose Brodeur to be his model for the French Captain, Gustav Gacon, General Passaga's personal aide. Paul Brodeur was an American of French-Canadian descent, who was born in Webster, Massachusetts. He spoke French before learning to speak English. Raised in several New England towns, he graduated from Harvard Dental School in 1917, went to France under the auspices of the Red Cross to treat refugee children, and served in the French Legion as an artillery officer. He was the perfect model for the mural, wearing his own blue French dress uniform, officer's cap, and tall leather boots. For many years, the uniform was carefully stored and prized by his wife and their sons, Paul Jr. and David.

During the Great Depression of the 1930s, Brodeur found it difficult to earn a living as an orthodontist, so he began taking commissions from institutions, such as Harvard University, Radcliffe College, and the Yale Medical School, to execute life-sized bas-relief portraits of various dignitaries and officials. Andrew, with his skill in anatomy and portraiture, assisted Brodeur in this endeavor. "He was a great help to my father," Paul Brodeur Jr. noted, during an interview in which he described the respectful, lasting friendship that is fondly remembered by the Brodeur family today.

During the 1920s, Brodeur's future wife, Sarah, was a beautiful actress with blue eyes and striking blonde hair. At the age of twenty-two, she posed as Andrew's model for the allegorical figure Columbia, gracing the left panel of the Hall of Valor mural. In this painted scene, Columbia is supported by the American eagle as she offers her sword to the aid of France, commemorating 150 years of friendship between the two nations.

David Brodeur, who lives near Gloucester, Massachusetts, not far from where the Andrews lived, tells of the touching relationship that existed between Paul Sr. and Sarah, and Richard and Lucy Andrew, to whom the Brodeurs brought comfort and support during the Andrews' waning years. It was David's letter written on December 18, 2001, to the Cape Ann Historical Society that brought our discovery team to the story of the long friendship between the Brodeur and Andrew families. In personal interviews he talked of his father (1884 – 1967), and he furnished the information about how his parents modeled for the Hall of Valor murals. His pleasure in having known Richard Andrew and his pride in owning some of Andrew's art was evident.

Sarah's sons, Paul Jr. and David, hold Andrew's artwork in high esteem. They treasure their collection of Andrew's paintings—especially his portrait of Paul Sr. —and remember Andrew with great affection and admiration. When asked what would best encapsulate the work of Richard Andrew, Paul Jr. replied, "My father always said that Richard Andrew was an exceptionally fine draughtsman and a wonderful portraitist with a singular eye for capturing the essence of his subject's expression."

Photographs: Paul A. Brodeur and Sarah B. Totten
Models for the Murals
Private Collection, Truro, Massachusetts

Photograph: *Richard Andrew*
Private Collection, Boston, Massachusetts

ALLEGORICAL PANELS
COLUMBIA AND THE EAGLE
GALLIA AND JOAN OF ARC

Photograph: *Hall of Valor: 104th Infantry*
Massachusetts State House, Boston

Oil on Canvas
111 x 41 in., 1927
Massachusetts State House
Boston

COLUMBIA AND THE EAGLE
Allegorical Panel on the left side of the Mural of the 104th Regiment

Columbia offers her sword to the aid of France to commemorate 150 years of friendship. She holds the service flag, which shows gold stars in memory of the heroes fallen in battle. The eagle represents the United States.

Oil on Canvas
111 x 44 in., 1927
Massachusetts State House
Boston

GALLIA AND JOAN OF ARC
Allegorical Panel on the right side of the Mural of the 104th Regiment

Gallia is the personification of France. In the mural, she is supported by Joan of Arc, the patron saint of patriotism. Gallia awards the wreath of honor to the valor of men of the 104th Regiment.

ARTIST FINDS PERFECT JOAN

Auburndale Girl Selected to Pose as Famous Maid---Chosen from More Than 1000

MISS MARIE LOUISE THOMAS

Boston Post
Saturday May 22, 1926

This announcement was made yesterday by Richard Andrew, noted Boston artist, commissioned to paint the memorial mural. He characterized Miss Thomas as the ideal conception of the famous Maid of Orleans, saying that from a physical and spiritual standpoint, the Auburndale girl compared favorably with the 15th century lass of history.

Joan was 18 years of age when she became her country's savior. Miss Thomas is 18. Joan was not a flapper type, but a sturdy feminine peasant of the fields. Miss Thomas is the same type, although she is American bred. Her parents hail from the soil of Domremy, France, that produced Joan. Again, Miss Thomas' weight and measurements are almost identical with those of the maid. She weighs 127 pounds, is five feet, two and a half inches, and has the same deep chest expansion.

Mr. Andrew describes Miss Thomas' hair as ash brown. Her eyes are a clear brown and are very large. Her nose is thin, straight and sensitive. Her cheekbones are broad and high. Her skin is fair and unblemished. She has never used rouge.

Muscles and a "Saint"

But, most important of all, declared the happy artist yesterday at his studio on Ipswich Street, *she has muscles, and a saint-like expression. What a remarkable combination. Her face is absolutely like that of a medieval saint, and yet, she has the* muscular body. Her arms and limbs are all muscle no superfluous fat. She is decidedly the type I had despaired of finding, and a beautiful type, and so unspoiled and unsophisticated.

Miss Thomas, who was present during the interview, smiles slightly. She is bashful and very shy. Although she admits she has studied with Ruth St. Denis and has done some barefoot dancing before the public, it appears that as yet she has not lost a certain quaint modesty. This is the first time she has ever posed for an artist. She loves books and animals.

I consider myself very fortunate in finding her, but if it was not for the Post, I should not have secured Miss Thomas. She is one of hundreds of girls who offered their services to me as a result of the Post Story. He explained referring to the story printed last Monday in the Post which told of the fact that the artist commissioned to paint the mural for the State House was unable to find a model suitable to represent Joan of Arc.

Offers Service Free

The girl's mother, Mrs. Albert Thomas, stated that she realized from the description given that her daughter was the type and called up Mr. Andrew, offering her daughter's services gratis because she felt that it would be a great honor to her daughter.

Didn't Want Professional

I never believed there was as much kindness in the world until this week when I discovered that the girls, who offered themselves as models, were absolutely unselfish. They wanted only to help. None of them sought personal glorification, money or fame. It was a beautiful demonstration, and I am most grateful to the Post.

I regretted that I was obliged to say, "No" to so many girls who came to see me. Few realize that the Joan of Arc type is difficult to find in America. You see Miss Thomas is a French girl though American born, and of course, so was Joan. That was the type I must have for my mural. Many of the flappers are lovely in their way, but they wouldn't do for that warrior maid with her saintly face.

Wears Bobbed Hair

Miss Thomas is built on much broader lines than the average miss of today, but strangely, though it may seem, she is, according to Mr. Andrew, much more graceful. There is a decided beauty and rhythm in her movements. Her limbs are well rounded, but they are sturdy and strong. However, her ankle tapers down gracefully. She has a short, wide foot, which is exceedingly well-formed. She wears 4C shoes. Her hands are fairly small and slightly broad, but they show a certain strength and firmness. Firmness and determination are also expressed in the line of her lovely red lips.

She wears her hair bobbed but not shingled, and it is parted in the center resembling the style Joan affected after she assumed the masculine warrior garb.

The Lookout
Charcoal and Chalk on Paper
8.75 x 24.25 in., 1927
Collection of James Dean

1931 State House Murals: A History of the Sixth Regiment

Boston War Murals

The Art Digest
November 15, 1931

Highlights in the history of the old Sixth Regiment of Massachusetts have been represented in a series of mural paintings by Richard Andrew, Boston artist, which have been unveiled in the Massachusetts State House. This Famous regiment according to the Boston Post, had its origin in the *Lexington Minute Men*, won honors in the Civil and Spanish Wars, and preserved its identity until the World War, when it became the 26th or Yankee Division. Soldiers in the uniforms of these wars have been painted in the end panels, and in the spaces between important historical events have been depicted.

The murals are grouped about a bronze statue of Roger Wolcott, Governor of Massachusetts during the Spanish War, which is the work of late Daniel Chester French. The Post: "Fresh and clean in color, admirably composed as well as accurate historically these new murals will add their full quota of beauty to the Hall of Valor."

The entire central wall behind the statue of Governor Wolcott is covered by murals honoring the men of the 6th Massachusetts Regiment.

The murals were donated to the Commonwealth by the Sixth Regiment Veterans Association. Their erection was authorized by a special act of the Legislature. The four paintings are located in the third floor corridor opposite the Chamber of the House of Representatives.

On the left of the statue of Governor Wolcott is a painting portraying the Massachusetts 6th regiment in an encounter with a mob in the streets of Baltimore April 19, 1861, on its way to protect the National Capitol. (Civil War)

The large mural on the right of the statue shows the landing of the Wakefield Company of the Regiment in Guanica, Porto Rico.* Colonel Edward J. Gihon was a captain of the Wakefield Company.

He posed for the artist, Richard Andrew, who portrayed him directing his troops as they disembarked from the gunboat "Gloucester" and the troopship "Yale" and charged upon the Spanish troops on the shore.

Governor Roger Wolcott
Bronze statue
Massachusetts State House, Boston

*The Spanish spelling and pronunciation Puerto Rico officially replaced the Latin form, Porto Rico, in 1932 to stress the Spanish cultural heritage of the majority of the island's population.

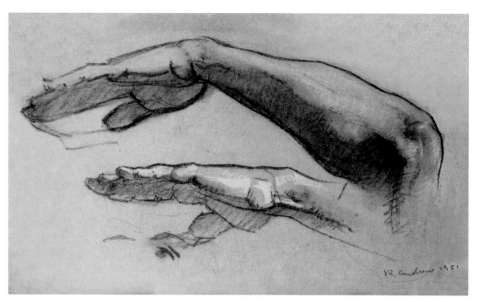

Lookout Study
18 x 24 in., 1931
Charcoal and Chalk on Paper
Private Collection, Derbyshire, Vermont

Soldier Study
Charcoal and Chalk on Paper
10 x 7.4 in., 1931
Private Collection, Boston, Massachusetts

Civil War Soldier
Charcoal and Chalk on Paper
10 x 7.4 in., 1931
Private Collection, Boston, Massachusetts

FOREWORD

THIS MEMORIAL IS DEDICATED TO THOSE LOYAL SONS OF MASSACHUSETTS WHO HAVE SERVED IN HER SIXTH REGIMENT IN THE FOUR GREAT WARS IN WHICH THIS COUNTRY HAS BEEN ENGAGED. MAY THEIR EXAMPLE BE AN INSPIRATION TO THOSE WHO READ THESE LINES BETTER TO SERVE THEIR COUNTRY AND THEIR GOD. ·THE WAR OF THE REVOLUTION· FROM THE INCOMPLETE RECORDS OF THIS WAR WE FIND THAT THE SIXTH MASSACHUSETTS REGIMENT EMERGED DURING THE YEAR 1778 FROM THE COMPANIES OF MINUTEMEN AND MILITIA FORMED BY THE STURDY PATRIOTS OF MIDDLESEX AND ADJOINING COUNTIES.

THE CIVIL WAR

THIS REGIMENT WAS THE FIRST BODY OF TROOPS TO RESPOND READY FOR SERVICE, TO THE FIRST CALL OF PRESIDENT LINCOLN FOR VOLUNTEERS, AND THE FIRST TO SHED ITS BLOOD. THREE TIMES THEY VOLUNTEERED FOR DUTY DURING THIS WAR. FIRST SERVICE, CALLED APRIL 15, 1861, REPORTED AT BOSTON APRIL 16, ENGAGED WITH BALTIMORE MOB APRIL 19, REACHED WASHINGTON APRIL 19 MUSTERED INTO UNITED STATES SERVICE APRIL 22, MUSTERED OUT AUGUST 2, 1861. A GREAT NUMBER OF THE REGIMENT IMMEDIATELY VOLUNTEERED FOR FURTHER DUTY WITH OTHER ORGANIZATIONS. SECOND SERVICE MUSTERED IN AUGUST 31, 1862, ENGAGEMENTS- ZUNI, DECEMBER 12, 1862, DESERTED HOUSE JANUARY 30, 1863, CARRSVILLE MAY 15, 1863, MUSTERED OUT JUNE 3, 1863. THIRD SERVICE, MUSTERED IN JULY 20, 1864 ON DUTY AT FORT DELAWARE MOST OF THIS ENLISTMENT, MUSTERED OUT OCTOBER 27, 1864.

1778 THE WAR OF THE REVOLUTION AND 1861 THE CIVIL WAR

The first of four murals commemorating the Sixth Massachusetts Regiment contain two long sections of text on the history of the regiment separated by two soldiers standing in uniform, one representing the Revolutionary War and one representing the Civil War.

Oil on Canvas
111 x 115 in., 1931
Massachusetts State House, Boston

Soldier Study
Charcoal and Chalk on Paper
16.4 x 15.2 in., 1931
Private Collection, Boston, Massachusetts

Figure Study
Charcoal and Chalk on Paper
19 x 24.75 in., 1931
Private Collection, Kensington, New Hampshire

Soldier Study
Charcoal on Paper
12 x 10 in., 1931
Private Collection, Derbyshire, Vermont

1861 THE CIVIL WAR

 The second mural depicts the April 19, 1861, encounter in Baltimore between the Sixth Regiment, on its way to protect the U.S. Capitol, and a group of protesters. The ensuing riot killed four men; they were the first to die in the Civil War. After suppressing the protesters, the Sixth Regiment continued on their march, becoming the first military unit to reach Washington later that day.

Oil on Canvas
111 x 149 in., 1931
Massachusetts State House, Boston

Subject: Col. Edward J. Gihon
Charcoal on Paper
15 x 14 in, 1931
Private Collection, Boston, Massachusetts

Soldier Study
Charcoal on Paper
10 x 25 in., 1931
Private Collection, Shrewsbury, Massachusetts

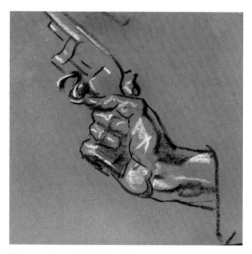

Charcoal and Chalk on Paper
10 x 10 in., 1931
Private Collection, Derbyshire, Vermont

Soldier Portrait
Charcoal and Chalk on Paper
10 x 7.5 in., 1931
Private Collection, Boston, Massachusetts

1898 THE SPANISH AMERICAN WAR

The third mural depicts the July 1898 arrival of the Sixth Regiment's Wakefield Company in Guanica, Puerto Rico during the Spanish American War.

Colonel Edward J. Gihon was captain of the Wakefield Company. He posed for the artist, who portrayed him directing his troops as they disembarked from the gunboat "Gloucester" and the troopship "Yale" and charged upon the Spanish troops waiting on the shore.

Oil on Canvas
111 in. x 149 in., 1931
Massachusetts State House, Boston

Soldier Studies
Charcoal and Chalk on Paper
15.5 x 25 in., 1931
Private Collection, Shrewsbury, Massachusetts

THE SPANISH WAR

AGAIN THE REGIMENT SHOWED ITS READINESS, AND IN RESPONSE TO PRESIDENT McKINLEY'S CALL FOR TROOPS, REPORTED AT FRAMINGHAM, MAY 6, 1898, RECRUITED TO WAR STRENGTH, AND MAY 13 WAS MUSTERED INTO UNITED STATES SERVICE FOR TWO YEARS. LEFT FOR CAMP ALGER, VIRGINIA, MAY 20. ORDERED FOR FOREIGN SERVICE AND EMBARKED AT CHARLESTON, SOUTH CAROLINA, JULY 8, ARRIVING AT SIBONEY CUBA, JULY 11. HELD IN RESERVE AT THE BATTLE OF SANTIAGO UNTIL ITS SURRENDER, THEN ORDERED TO PORTO RICO AS PART OF THE EXPEDITION THAT CAPTURED THAT ISLAND. ENGAGED AT GUANICA AND YAUCO ROAD. THEN SERVED IN THE ARMY OF OCCUPATION UNTIL ORDERED HOME. SAILED FROM SAN JUAN OCTOBER 21, ARRIVING IN BOSTON OCTOBER 29. MUSTERED OUT AT BOSTON JANUARY 21, 1899.

THE WORLD WAR

THE REGIMENT RESPONDED TO THE FIRST CALL FOR TROOPS IN THE WORLD WAR, REPORTING MARCH 30, 1917, TO GUARD PUBLIC UTILITIES. ORDERED TO FRAMINGHAM THEN TO CAMP DEVENS, DRAFTED INTO THE UNITED STATES SERVICE AUGUST 5, ORDERED TO WESTFIELD, WHERE 1600 OFFICERS AND MEN WERE ASSIGNED TO VARIOUS UNITS OF THE 26TH (Y.D.) DIVISION, WITH WHICH GALLANT ORGANIZATION THEY SERVED WITH DISTINCTION IN THE A.E.F. THE REMAINING OFFICERS AND MEN SERVED IN THE A.E.F. WITH GREAT CREDIT IN THE 4TH PIONEERS AND 372ND INFANTRY.

1898 THE SPANISH AMERICAN WAR AND 1917 THE WORLD WAR

The last of the four murals commemorates the history of the regiment separated by two soldiers standing in uniform, one representing the Spanish American War and one representing World War I.

Oil on Canvas
111 x 115 in., 1931
Massachusetts State House, Boston

EXERCISES AT UNVEILING

OCTOBER 31, 1931

SELECTION "America"	BAND
INVOCATION	REV. WILLIAM F. DUSSEAULT
UNVEILING *America the Beautiful*	MISS PRISCILLA H. DARLING
PRESENTATION TO THE COMMONWEALTH	COL. WARREN E. SWEETSER
ACCEPTANCE FOR THE COMMONWEALTH *Gen. Agnew*	GOV. JOSEPH B. ELY
DEDICATORY ADDRESS	SENATOR DAVID I. WALSH
CLOSING SELECTION "The Star Spangled Banner"	BAND

We gratefully acknowledge the assistance given us by the following friends in the preparation of this Memorial:

The Massachusetts Legislature in granting permission to us to place the Memorial in the State House.
The Massachusetts Art Commission for its aid and advice.
Ex-President Calvin Coolidge for his suggestions regarding the inscription.
Mr. Fred W. Cross for his assistance in compiling records.
And to the many other friends who have aided us in various ways.
And finally to Mr. Richard Andrew, our artist, to whom much of the credit is due for the conception and execution of this beautiful Memorial.

A Visit to the Massachusetts State House in the 21st Century

Photo Courtesy of the Massachusetts Art Commission

The Massachusetts State House welcomes its visitors with dignity and respect. It is a combination of architectural elegance and recorded history. The beautiful marble concourse on the third and principal floor certainly falls within both categories. On July 4, 1795, the surviving fathers of the Revolutionary War were on hand to enshrine the ideal Commonwealth in a graceful seat of government designed by Charles Bulfinch. Governor Samuel Adams and Paul Revere laid the cornerstone.

Charles Bulfinch (1763-1844), the most famous architect in the early days of our nation, influenced the character and beauty of America. He was educated at Harvard University and traveled throughout Europe between 1785 and 1787. His mentors were Thomas Jefferson and Sir Christopher Wren. He designed the Massachusetts State House with the devotion of a Boston native, and set an architectural sense of neoclassical beauty and simplicity not surpassed to this day.

According to the book, *The State House*, at the dedication ceremony of Richard Andrew's mural depicting the 104th Infantry Division on April 30, 1927, Governor Alvan T. Fuller said, "I have heard the Lord Chief Justice of England, John Duke Lord Coleridge, quoted as saying, 'Far the most beautiful city in America, as far as I have seen, is Boston, and the State House is the most beautiful in the country. At Washington, at Albany, at Chicago, and elsewhere, you see much grander and more costly structures. But this is in perfect taste and proportion. Every interspace the right size, every molding of the noblest type...The situation is noble and has been made the best of.'"

"In this historic building we have mural/paintings. Not far from these pictures are the offices of the Governor of the Commonwealth. Just across the corridor is the chamber of the House of Representatives. Down another corridor is the old chamber where the Senate sits. The Secretary of the Commonwealth and the other constitutional officers have their offices nearby." Governor of the Commonwealth of Massachusetts, Alvan T. Fuller, continued, "I believe that those who may occupy those offices in the years to come will, by the presence of this pictured scene, be better citizens for it. I believe that the throngs of people, children and their parents, who yearly visit this State House, will carry home with them a finer and a more vigorous love of Massachusetts, from the sight here represented of the honor done sons of the State in a time that tried men's souls."

   To walk through these corridors of history today is more inspiring than even Governor Fuller could have predicted. There is a quick pace of activity, an intensity of purpose that thrills those of us who depend on the legislators to protect and see to it that the future is bright for all.

The Bulfinch design of the Massachusetts State House, with its golden dome and red brick siding, is stately and yet in keeping with the city and its other buildings. The legislative third floor can be seen as one ascends the marble staircase with its mahogany railings. Three floors are visible as they are situated around an open atrium; each floor is decorated with half walls of historic ironwork supported by Corinthian columns. The lighting is bright and gives one a sense of optimism.

The third floor is where the legislature considers its historic business. On any given day you will see conversations taking place between legislators—not light banter, but a smile and a handshake now and then. The roll call is impressive. A man of medium height who has preserved for us all the historic announcements of readiness to vote, peals out "ROLL CALL! ROLL CALL!" in a deep and resonate voice that echoes throughout the corridors.

It is here that the paintings of Richard Andrew fascinate many who visit the Massachusetts State House. It is here that the soldiers of the 104th Infantry Regiment, the Revolutionary War, the Spanish American War, the Civil War, and World War I are honored.

The paintings are bright and clean, in such excellent condition that you might think they had been painted yesterday. Dedicated in 1927 and 1931, Richard Andrew's murals continue to inspire and delight Massachusetts State House visitors.

Part III: The Man and His Art

For a complete list of artwork, see page 160.

Self-portrait, 1933
Oil on Canvas
20 x 25 in.
Courtesy of the Whistler House Museum of Art,
Lowell Art Association, Inc.
Gift of the Artist

"Oh yes, young men go into painting just as they always have gone; some because they think they can have a pleasant life, and others because the urge will not allow them to stay out. If the urge is strong enough, you can't stop a young man. He simply will do what the urge says and the world is really as hungry for beauty as it ever was."

-R. Andrew, June 5, 1921

GIRL WITH A LANTERN

Subject: Edwina Andrew
Oil on Canvas
19.5 x 23.5 in., 1917
Private Collection, New Hampshire
*See Edwina's story on page 53.

INTRODUCTION

It has been a journey of joy to travel the path of Richard Andrew's life and times (1869-1956). As a lecturer, art educator, writer, sculptor, printmaker, and artist, his talents and deeply-felt philosophy about painting exhibited a passion and urge to express himself perfectly. This is vividly depicted in the hundreds of studies found during the search and discovery for this book.

The breadth of Richard Andrew's prodigious career has developed profound respect and sheer awe at what we, today, experience as admirers of this artist, more than fifty years after his death.

> *The canvas entitled "The Schoolgirl" represents a young girl just awakening to the great facts of life and personality. "It should also represent the significance of a certain state of adolescence and should stand for any and all youth. Then it will be of interest to future generations when both sitter and painter have ceased to live."*
>
> -Richard Andrew
> *See pg. 103.*

You will see in the following pages portraits entitled "The Schoolgirl," "The Girl Scout," "The Blueberry Girl," "J.C.S. Andrew," "The Football Player," and more. Inherent in each portrait is an expression of a period of life. Additionally, there are inspiring landscapes, coastal views, marine, and still life paintings. These photographs have been gathered from proud owners of Richard Andrew's paintings all over the United States.

Harbor
Watercolor on Paper
12 x 8.5 in., 1890
Private Collection, New Hampshire

From lectures, writings, and interviews Richard Andrew has shared his philosophical principles:

> The desire to reach perfection, no matter how long or how hard, is basic to success.
>
> The power to produce so fine a canvas that it will be preserved for generations to come.
>
> The rugged truth, the artistic quality and that powerful interpretation of his canvas will make a fine artist.
>
> The chief thing needed is insight and sincerity and the understanding of what things mean.
>
> Excellence of a sense of design, form and draughtsmanship is essential.
>
> Intellectual command of the theme is the basic tenet prior to putting brush to canvas.

Implicit in understanding Richard Andrew's views on painting is an article published in 1921 when, as a prominent Boston artist, he was asked to be interviewed by a staff writer of *The Boston Herald*, M. J. Curl, for a series called, "Boston Artists and Sculptors in Intimate Talks." We are fortunate to be able to read Richard Andrew's most personal thoughts.

> *"The problem before the young artist is to catch the power to make his canvas so fine that people watch over it and preserve it against the inevitable ravages of time."*
>
> -Richard Andrew
> See pg. 103.

In His Own Words
Boston Artists and Sculptors in Intimate Talks

By M.J. Curl

Boston Sunday Herald
June 5, 1921, Section E pg. 6

Photograph by Bachrach
RICHARD ANDREW

It is impossible to put into words the chief thing needed by the painter today, says Mr. Richard Andrew, instructor in painting at the Massachusetts Normal Art School. To the public it would be to have something to say. But the artist detests that phrase because he does not appeal through the ear but through the eye, and he has nothing to "say" or to "tell" but something to show. In this the chief thing needed today is insight and sincerity. In Boston we have many painters who show the finest kind of technical knowledge and ability. We also find a real beauty in the ideas they express, but the ability to image ideas of this nature is much less frequent than the ability to embody the obvious aspect of things by the skillful application of paint-to-canvas.

A person can learn the craft of painting, how to draw correctly and how to apply his paint well, but it is another matter to open that person's eyes to the significance of what he sees. If a painter really has a message to deliver to his canvas, he can discover the means to express it. I am astonished at the quickness with which a student can learn the mechanics of the profession—correct draughtsmanship and the putting on of paint.

It is different with ideas.

Understanding the Best Thing

In my teaching I used to pay more attention to the mechanics of the problem. Judged by the results, the best thing, to my mind, to do for students is to show them the significance of the subjects of their painting, to open their eyes wide to the world around them. If they really see, really understand the meaning of what they are attempting to represent or suggest in their work, I seem to have found them able to make the painting with comparable success. Ruskin said a great deal of truth in the remark that great art is never the result of large effort by a small man but rather occurs without effort by a big man. The big man, the man with the idea, the man who has done much thinking before he paints, about the world and the relations of things, is the one who, if his hand has been trained reasonably, will make the better pictures. My experience with students leads me to believe that this is the best thing to do for them and I am more and more trying to do it.

When you find an American Artist with the ability to draw adequately and also the insight and understanding of what things mean, you get strong work. Take Winslow Homer's paintings of the wilderness. He lived in Maine, knew the life, understood the problems of the point of view of the men who faced the wilderness and tamed it for human use. Consequently, from his very isolation and opportunity to think things over and really comprehend them, along with the ability to draw, he made a real interpretation of a whole phase of American life, and made it soundly and well.

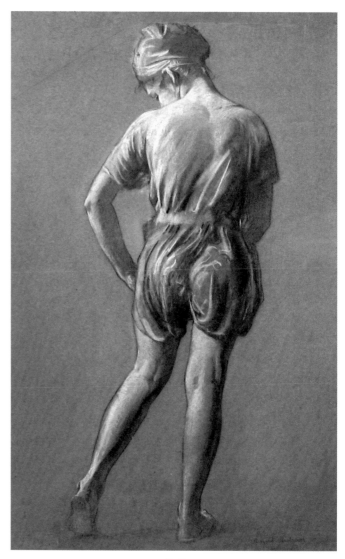

Ruth
Pastel on Paper
13.5 x 22 in.
Private Collection, Boston, Massachusetts

The "Innocent Eye" Is Fading

Our shibboleths are changing: make it like has not the force it once had. We discovered that the phase meant all things to all men. We are still hearing, especially here in Boston, about the "innocent eye." The phrase means that the painter merely reproduces on his canvas the exact image that he discovers on the retina of his eye. Now in the first place, this is impossible—if you don't believe it, just try sometime to make the skin of an orange lie flat; you'll have the same problem as in making the concave retinal image lie out on a flat canvas.

The "innocent eye" hardly demanded that the painter find the significance of things— it demanded good eyesight. Now we are hoping for more than that.

The spiritual significance appears in such painting as Rembrandt made. He always saw more than so much material before him. Take the painting of that old woman cleaning her finger nails—there you have, so far as the mere "innocent eye" would go, a human being of no great pretension concerned with the humble task of keeping her body clean. Rembrandt saw more than that: he discovered the significance—and the painting is so much the better for it.

To come back to the "innocent eye"—it is a very sophisticated thing because it requires a fine training to recognize the retinal image apart from everything else. It will always contribute its share to the work of the painter, but more. Most of us have two eyes, each with its own retinal image. It will be an innocent person indeed, who will decide which of his eyes is the more innocent and consequently which image he should copy, provided, as we have said, he could do that. No, I am afraid that the sense of range or depth afforded the mind by the vision of both eyes will have to be taken into account.

No Great American Masters of the Nude

That sense of distance, of volume, which every normal person acquired early in his boyhood, does not desert us and will have to be reckoned with in drawing, in painting and in sculpture. Rodin in his talks has explained as well as it can be done in words what a clarifying principle it was for him. To draw in terms of volume is no new thing: Michael Angelo drew thus, and others have done the same thing. Painting gains in power by a recognition of this, too. For instance, take a look at the head of Aesop by Velasquez—more than the "innocent eye" was busy there.

Such a discussion as took place between Benvenuto Cellini and a rival concerning the rival's statue appearing like a bag of melons, so far as the variety of its component forms went, could never have been founded on the mere observation of the "innocent eye."

Nude
Pastel on Paper
Private Collection, Truro, Massachusetts

Many an American painter would fail to catch the point of Cellini's discussion today. This may explain to some extent the poor draughtsmanship that is far too often seen today—with notable exceptions. How easily we are satisfied with poor draughtsmanship! We have been criticized by the Europeans for that. And that is why since the human body is the most difficult thing to represent, we have no great masters of the nude in this country. The nude as the more or less agreeable portrayal of some individual model has a certain value as an exercise for the painter, but it has more value to him than to anyone else. The use of the nude as an ultimate shape in the other way is almost entirely foreign to us and I say this even with our mural painters in mind. In the nude, those great varieties of the component forms and of the complexity of their design coupled with the transitions from rest to action in the same figure which may show the physical character in a nicety become in the hands of a master the most subtle language of art.

Photography Has Had Large Effect

Some, turning away from school guidance and even from nature, say paint as you feel. In the last analysis, yes, but, as our Hunt would say, do base it upon a possibility. Painting as one feels easily may run him into difficulties. There are great enough differences in the way people see, let alone the greater differences in the way they feel.

The danger of being unintelligible is sufficient to affright a thinking person. The painter has to compete today as never before. In his own field the illustrator has a large advantage with the public. Photography with the hearts of chemical reproduction and the movies, draws people from the picture galleries. Today many a mediocre portrait painter is outshone by the artist photographer.

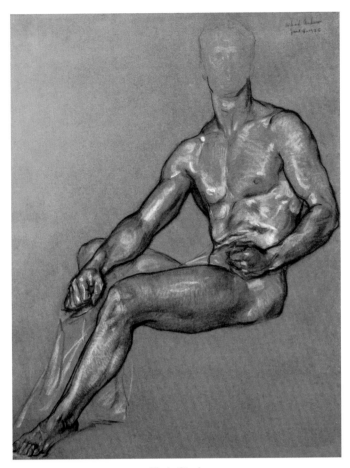

Nude Study
Charcoal on Paper
13 x 16 in., 1935
Private Collection, Franconia, New Hampshire

Many a photograph displays more of the personality of the sitter than the average portrait in oil. On the whole the effect of the photograph has been away from the generalized likeness toward the intense realization of actual details. That is not a bad thing and it has compelled many a painter to make a better likeness. Not that portraits should imitate photographs; merely that painters have been challenged in the public favor.

The moving picture is bound to have a large effect on painting—the dynamic picture against the static. What a compression of interests of vitality, the static painting will be compelled to employ if it is to hold its due share of attention. Of course, modern interest will tend to clear the field of all persons and things not essential to the art of painting. Waste of effort tends to disappear. But no European country would tolerate the waste of energy of those trained in the arts that is going on here today for lack of intelligent patronage or direction.

The Problem of the Young Man

Out of it all, I think we can say the best does survive, and that best in our country has been very fine and bids fair, I think, to be as fine in the future. In spite of certain influences to the contrary, now as in the past, it will pay to invest, to look at from that point of view, in good American paintings. Today the problem of the young man who wishes to enter the profession of painting is more interesting than ever before. Photographs and moving pictures are bound to crowd out the weaker men, just as the advertising and illustrating call of the magazines and other mediums in drawing many fine artists out of the ranks of the painters. Some weaker students will stay in the older form simply because they have no response to anything but the path of least resistance. Some of our very strong men in the schools are going over into advertising work. As to the real painter, the man who is called, as it were, nothing short of death can divert him from his path.

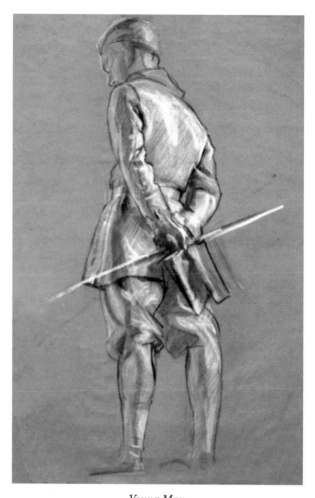

Young Man
Pastel on Paper
18 x 24 in.
Private Collection, Derbyshire, Vermont

The young man has always had to wait. Chavannes, who painted the decorations in the Public Library, was 40 years old before he was recognized. He had been doing fine work for years, but not till then did he make an impression. Once recognized, he was sure of his future. Millet, who might have done mural work, did not receive his commissions from the government until he was almost at the end of his life, and he died without seeing them accomplished, if even drawn. In some ways Boston is a less likely place for the young painter than either New York or the Middle West. Many of my students who have gone to New York have found plenty of commissions. They seem to be busy and successful. The Middle West is calling strongly these days for young men to come and take up the work there.

Oh yes, young men go into painting just as they have always gone; some because they think they can have a pleasant life, and others because the urge will not allow them to stay out. If the urge is strong enough, you can't stop a young man. He simply will do what the urge says, and the world is really as hungry for beauty as it ever was. But the problem before the young man is a large one. When I was a student in Paris it was said that in the city were 12,000 painters. It is inconceivable that every one of these painters made a fine picture every year. What do all these painters do? Where do all these paintings go? It really is a blessing that in the course of a lifetime canvas decays and paintings have to go to the scrap heap if not cared for. Even the old masters are subject to ravages.

Building a Fishing Schooner
Etching with Gouache
Private Collection, San Francisco, California

Every once in a while an old canvas has to be relined or stripped from the cloth just as you would peel a photographic film from the glass and then it is pasted upon a new canvas. Only in that way are we able to keep them. The problem before the young artist is to catch the power to make his canvas so fine that people watch over it and preserve it against the inevitable ravages of time. Mr. Andrew has recently had the honor of the first honorable mention at the Buffalo exhibit of paintings. His canvas to secure this honor was entitled "The Schoolgirl" and represents a young girl just awakening to the great facts of life and personality. He declares that such a canvas should be more than a transcript of the sitter. It should also represent the significance of a certain state of adolescence that should stand for any and all youth. Then it will be of interest to future generations when both sitter and painter have ceased to live.

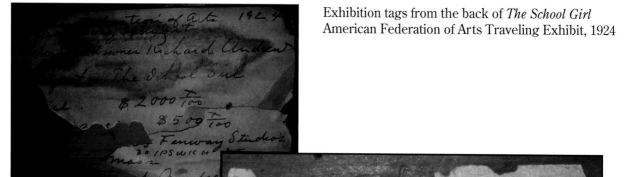

Exhibition tags from the back of *The School Girl*
American Federation of Arts Traveling Exhibit, 1924

Self-portrait
"To My Good Friend, Anton"
Oil on Canvas
Brandywine Museum, Chadds Ford, Pennsylvania

THE SCHOOL GIRL

Painted in approximately 1917, this painting was shown widely through the American Federation of Art traveling exhibition in 1924. The subject of "The School Girl" was Marguerite Andrew, niece of the artist. She returned from her home in Joplin, Missouri, as a ten-year old, and was raised by her maternal relatives, the Akeroyds, in Roxbury, Massachusetts. She graduated from Peter Bent Brigham Hospital in Boston, and was a fine nurse. Richard Andrew frequently used her as a model for his paintings. These portraits included, "The School Girl" and "The Blueberry Girl" which have been shown in exhibitions in the United States and abroad.

NEW YORK TIMES
Feb. 16, 1919

New York Times Magazine
pg. 72

Pennsylvania Academy's Annual Exhibition
Art at Home and Abroad

"The Schoolgirl," by Richard Andrew, has plastic precision and a richness of light and shade that recall the virtues of the seventeenth century Dutchmen. The portrait might have been painted by one of them, by one of the best of them, yet the type and vision are modern enough. It is the kind of painting that interests you in the problems of height and weight and character, and that soothes your mind with its suggestions of stability and repose yet it has the indispensable movement of life.

THE FINE ARTS
By W.H.D.

Boston Evening Transcript
29 Oct. 1918

Mr. Andrew's Pictures

His is the First One Man Show at the Guild, 16 Newbury St. was opened yesterday with the private view of an exhibition of paintings by Richard Andrew.

...The School Girl is also felicitious in the matter of poser arrangement of the shadow of the hat falling over the upper part of the face.

Exhibitions:
Guild of Boston Artists: 1918
Pennsylvania Academy of Fine Arts: 1919
Art Institute of Chicago: 1924

Subject: Marguerite Andrew
Oil on Canvas
33.5 x 39 in., c. 1917
Private Collection, Edmeston, New York

THE BLUEBERRY GIRL

THE FINE ARTS
by W.H.D.

Boston Evening Transcript
29 Oct. 1918

The season of the one-man shows at the Guild Gallery, 6 Newbury St., was opened with a private view of an exhibition of paintings by Richard Andrew.

The Blueberry Girl is one of the most vital heads, animated, gay, and spirited.

Subject: Marguerite Andrew
Oil on Canvas
28.5 x 35.5 in., c. 1918
Private Collection, Edmeston, New York

Exhibitions:
Guild of Boston Artists: 1918
Art Institute of Chicago: 1923

Portrait Group

Subjects: Ruth Andrew, Minnie Maud Andrew, Helen Andrew
Oil on Canvas
52 x 58 in., 1918
Private Collection, Lower Newton Falls, Massachusetts

Boston Evening Transcript
29 Oct. 1918

Mr. Andrew's Pictures

His is the First One Man Show of the year at the Gallery of the Guild of Boston Artists

The season of one man shows at the Guild Gallery, 16 Newbury St., was opened yesterday with the private view of an exhibition of paintings by Richard Andrew.

In his most important example of this genre, (portraits), the group of a mother and her two daughters, hung in the center of the far wall, he utilizes with success his familiarity with decorative principles which are often and should be oftener, employed in portraiture.

This portrait group of three figures is on a very high key, the lighting being unusually bright, the background a very light gray wall, and the costumes, summer gowns of light, cool colors, whites, grays, mauves, pale blues and lilacs. The mother and her two young daughters are seated on a divan in an obviously arranged grouping, which brings the heads very nearly the same level and in the same focus; and to obviate the horizontal effect of the heads, there is a dark-toned framed tray of Oriental lacquer-work hung on the wall just behind and a little above the row of heads, performing a pyramidal design. The heads are very well painted and excellently characterized, bringing out the family resemblance.

The Football Player

Nathaniel James Andrew II, born on July 17, 1886, and the subject of "The Football Player," was seventeen years younger than his brother, Richard, who idolized him. The many portraits of him have made their owners proud and protective of these works.

"Buster," as he was called, lived a large part of his life in Colorado and Missouri, where in partnership with his brother, Robert, he owned and operated silver and lead mines. Colorful stories of mining life during the early 1900s are part of the family lore.

Exhibitions:
Pennsylvania Academy of Fine Arts: 1905
Art Institute of Chicago: 1906
Cornell University Four Man Exhibition: 1908
Guild of Boston Artists: 1918

The Football Player
Oil on Canvas
32 x 47 in.
Private Collection, New Hampshire

The Silver Miners
Etching
Private Collection, San Francisco, California

MOTHER AND DAUGHTER
Subjects: Agnes and Minnie Andrew
Oil on Canvas
29 x 32 in.
Private Collection, Norwich, Vermont

LADY IN BLACK FURS

Subject: Minnie Maud Andrew
Guild of Boston Artists
Exhibition: 1918
Oil on Canvas
24 x 32.5 in.
Private Collection, Norwich, Vermont

Minnie Maud Andrew, the subject of "Girl in Black" and "Lady in Black Furs," was a graduate of Massachusetts School of Art, and was Richard Andrew's only sister. She devoted her life to raising her nieces, Ruth and Helen Andrew. She was called by subsequent generations of children "Ninnie," and was dearly loved by all.

J. C. S. ANDREW

THE FINE ARTS
By W.H.D.

Boston Evening Transcript
16 Nov. 1920
Pt. 2, p. 13

The Guild of Boston Artists opened its season of one-man-exhibitions yesterday with a private view of the collection of paintings by Richard Andrew, in a gallery, 162 Newbury St.

The interest of the occasion thus centers to a considerable degree in the portraits. That of the painter's brother, Professor J.C. S. Andrew of the Army Educational Corps in his uniform, is new, and shows him at full length, standing, in a position which is a rather happy combination of military bearing and of ease and naturalness. As in all his portraits, Mr. Andrew promptly asserts his strong sense of form and gives the observer immediate assurance of this sound and capable draftsmanship. He communicates with integrity and sincerity his admirable grasp of reality and intellectual command of his theme.

JOHN CHARLES STATES ANDREW
Oil on Canvas
20.25 x 33 in.
Private Collection, New Hampshire

John Charles States Andrew was a professor of religion at Boston University and a good friend of the president, Dr. Marsh. He lived in a brownstone on Beacon Hill in Brookline, Massachusetts until his death in 1954. Uncle Charlie, as he was known to his family, gave support and kindness to everyone he knew. One of his great nieces remembers how, with great fanfare, he always found a silver dollar for each visiting youngster in the family.

J.C.S. Andrew
Oil on Canvas
48 x 84 in.
Private Collection, San Francisco, California

Exhibitions:
Guild of Boston Artists: 1918, 1919, 1920
Pennsylvania Academy of Fine Arts: 1905, 1923

Boston Evening Transcript
12 Mar 1912

Andrew's "Girl in Black"

The outstanding feature of His One Man Show at the Copley Gallery, where this artist proves that he is to be classed among the coming men.

Because it has positive and serious qualities, which set it apart, and give it distinction, Richard Andrew's portrait of a "Girl in Black" at the Copley Gallery 161 Newbury St. is the outstanding feature of his exhibition. Beautiful and worthy of unqualified praise, as art, it has defects that may not be overlooked entirely, and the painter has not wholley succeeded in the effort it has cost him.

In this portrait the fine things are the painting of the arms, the head, neck, shoulders, and the black dress, all of which are executed with uncommon ability and in parts with astonishing delicacy, beauty and brilliancy. The contrast of the very fine black in the dress with the luminous flesh tones which come next to it is one of the delightful features of the work. The expression of character in the head and the movement of the figure is also set down as one of the unusual achievements connected with this serious effort.

Exhibitions:
McDowell Club of New York: 1912
Copley Gallery: 1912, 1941

GIRL IN BLACK

Subject: Minnie Maud Andrew
Oil on Canvas
59 x 50.3 in.
Private Collection, Boston, Massachusetts

My Father

THE FINE ARTS
By W.H.D.

Boston Evening Transcript
16 Nov. 1920
Pt. 2 p 13

Pictures by Mr. Andrew

First-Rate Portraits, Marine Pieces and
Landscapes, in First of the Guild's One Man
Exhibitions

The Guild of Boston Artists opened its season
of one-man exhibitions yesterday afternoon—
a month later than usual—with a private view
of the collection of paintings by Richard
Andrew, in the gallery, 162 Newbury street.

...The most interesting and penetrating
piece of work in the way of a portrait is the
painting of the artist's father. It is evident
that the subjective element in this canvas
has been wholly unconscious, and that it
is on this account all the more genuine and
valid. The work is done with infinite care,
and a maximum of what we are pleased to
call the artistic conscience. The drawing and
modeling of the fine head and the expressive
hands are all that could be desired. There is
a beautiful sanity and completeness in this
portrait. It must be what President Emeritus
Eliot calls one of the durable satisfactions of
life to be able to paint a portrait of a father in
this manner.

Exhibitions:
Guild of Boston Artists: 1919
Copley Gallery: 1941

Subject: John Andrew
Oil on Canvas
39 x 45 in., 1909
Private Collection, New Hampshire

CLARA

CYNTHIA

Oil on Canvas
24.5 x 29.5 in.
Private Collection, New Hampshire

Cynthia Hollis often wore a high-necked dress and a veil to cover the goiter which was distracting to her beautiful face. A kind, well-educated woman, she was devoted to her family, and is remembered with respect. Her husband called her his beloved "Tinnie."

Clara Hollis, the younger sister of Cynthia, died of tuberculosis within months of the completion of this portrait.

Oil on Canvas
31 x 48 in.
Private Collection, New Hampshire

Emil Christian Hammer, Danish Consulate at the Port of Boston (1859-1894), is shown here under the tent, painting. A remarkable business man, he started the Walworth Manufacturing Company and the Walworth Clock Company in Waltham, Massachusetts. His other broad business interests were impressive. At his death in 1894, Mr. Hammer was worth $10 million. His wife, Martha Payne Hollis, inherited this fortune.

Subsequently, Cynthia Hollis, her daughter and the beloved stepdaughter of Emil Hammer, was given the responsibility of managing this money. She became one of Boston's great philanthropists. Emil Hammer and Richard Andrew were very close friends. They were drawn together by their mutual love of art and significant artistic talents. Richard Andrew painted his friend while on an outing in the woods.

EMIL CHRISTIAN HAMMER

Watercolor on Paper
13.5 x 19 in.
Private Collection, New Hampshire

Photograph: *Richard Andrew in His Studio*
Private Collection, Franconia, New Hampshire

Girl in the Black Hat

Subject: Ruth Andrew
Art Institute of Chicago
Exhibition: 1924
Oil on Canvas, 24.5 x 32.7 in.
Private Collection, Boston, Massachusetts

The "Girl in the Black Hat" was produced over many months. Richard Andrew's letters regarding painting sessions show this tender, thoughtful artist, who was solicitous of his sitter regarding the "cold studio" and "difficulty of travel."

Ruth, born in 1903, graduated from Pratt Institute in 1926. She taught art, was an interior decorator, and raised four children alone while her husband was fighting in World War II.

CAPTAIN ROBERT C. DEAN

Oil on Canvas
24 x 28.5 in., 1940
Private Collection, Shrewsbury, Massachusetts

This portrait of Captain Robert Dean was completed in 1940. Mr. Philip Hofer, curator of Harvard College Library, mentioned in a letter to Andrew, "I can safely say that I admire your work (Richard Andrew's) and feel it is very real, very American." Captain Dean became a Brigadier General after World War II for his leadership in the front lines. Pride in his country was obvious to all who knew him.

A great admirer of Richard Andrew, Dean was an architect in Boston's Perry, Shaw, Hepburn, Kehoe, & Dean firm. An artist in his own right, Dean was credited with leadership in the reconstruction of Colonial Williamsburg and the planning and construction of Furman University, among other notable architectural achievements.

Portrait in Pink

Subject: Marian Goddard
Oil on Board
15.25 x 19.5 in., 1944
Private Collection, Edmeston, New York

In 1944 when Richard Andrew was seventy-five, he called his great-niece, Marian Goddard, to come to Gloucester from Hartford, Connecticut, for a sitting. She was then seventeen years of age, and she remembers well the studio and the intensity of the artist. She didn't hear anything more from him until 1952 when the study was sent as a gift to her. It was nice, but later put on a shelf and forgotten.

On an impromptu trip to Derbyshire, Vermont in 2006, to follow up on a lead to find more of Richard Andrew's art, this painting sat with more than a hundred sketches and studies. The owner of the painting said softly, "I have always loved that painting and now I know who she is." This oil painting was united with the sitter, the author of this book, sixty-two years later!

IN THE ROUND WINDOW

Subject: Marguerite Andrew
Oil on Board
13.75 x 19.75 in., 1928
Private Collection, Edmeston, New York

LUCY CHOATE PEW ANDREW

Model for "Autumn"
Oil on Canvas
Dimensions
Private Collection, Roanoke, Virginia

Lucy Choate Pew Andrew, born and raised in Gloucester, Massachusetts, was often the model for her husband's paintings. Married for more than fifty years, theirs was a marriage of devotion and discipline, as Richard Andrew's urge to paint was so great as to dominate their lives. Lucy was an intelligent, well-read woman whose skills as a wife and mate helped Andrew grow to the height of his profession. She is remembered with love and great respect.

THE GIRL SCOUT

Subject: Ruth Andrew
Guild of Boston Artists
Exhibition: 1918
Oil on Canvas
35.25 x 28.5 in.
Private Collection, Massachusetts

The painting of his niece, Ruth Andrew, as a "Girl Scout" echoes Richard Andrew's consistent principles in honoring the stages in life. Always a patriotic man, this portrait represents his heartfelt feelings about character building in young people.

GIRL SCOUT PROMISE

On my honor, I will try:
To serve God and my country,
To help people at all times,
And to live by the Girl Scout Law.

LUCY

Pastel on Paper
9.5 x 13.5 in.
Private Collection, Franconia, New Hampshire

AUTUMN

THE FINE ARTS
Boston Evening Transcript
12 Mar 1912

Of much importance...is the large decoration placed at the end of the gallery and entitled "Autumn." There are those who will judge this mural decoration to be possibly the more important of the two works. It is certainly the most creditable achievement in the field of decorative art for a man of limited experience in this line of Mr. Andrew. Some of the figures are extremely well posed and are not wanting in a certain air of almost classic nobility and "the grand style." This is especially true of the woman at the right. The tone, the color, the accessories, such as the autumn fruits and vegetables so appropriately strewn about the foreground, all these are well thought out and excellently executed, and, what is still more important, the hands together with the fine effect of unity, to which both its design and its color materially contribute.

Autumn Sketch
Model: Nathaniel Andrew
Charcoal on Paper
4.5 x 6.5 in.
Private Collection, Derbyshire, Vermont

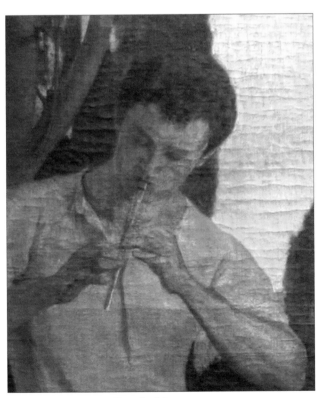

Detail of *Autumn*

Autumn Exhibitions:
Pennsylvania Academy of Fine Arts: 1911
Art Institute of Chicago: 1911
Biennial Exhibition: Washington DC: 1912
McDowell Club, New York: 1912
Copley Gallery, Boston: 1941

GLOUCESTER DAILY TRIBUNE
16 Oct. 1913

A painting of much importance and also of great local interest that has captured admirers of art is a large decoration called, "Autumn," a certainly most creditable achievement of décorative art.

Mr. Andrew's "Autumn" with its young man and two women in modern costume, with its display of humble but artistically dignified fruits of the season, strikes one as a work worthy of comparison with many decorations which have stood the test of time.

This decoration "Autumn," should be of special interest to the residents of Gloucester, because many of the "studies" were made in the vicinity of Wolf Hill. In order to obtain the unusual effect of moonrise and sunset after-glow upon the water, Mr. Andrew would row over to Russ' Island, opposite Wolf Hill and paint from there, on a hill. He also worked out of doors in order to get the reflections absolutely correct in tone, value and color.

Autumn Study
Model: Minnie Maud Andrew
Oil on Board
20 x 30 in.
Private Collection,
Lower Newton Falls, Massachusetts

In 2008, the third, fourth, and fifth generation descendents of Richard Andrew donated the necessary funding to have the mural "Autumn" restored. The mural is proudly displayed in Furman University's James B. Duke Library.

AUTUMN

Oil on Canvas
74.25 x 88.25 in., c. 1912
Furman University, Greenville, South Carolina

AUTUMN MOUNTAIN LANDSCAPE

Oil on Canvas
36 x 28 in.
Private Collection, Edmeston, New York

RUTH ANDREW
Oil on Board
22 x 29.5 in.
Private Collection, Lower Newton Falls, Massachusetts

HELEN

Oil on Canvas
9.5 x 13.5
Private Collection, Rochester, New York

CHERRIES

Oil on Canvas
35 x 27.5 in.
Private Collection, Edmeston, New York

MOUNT CHOCORUA, NEW HAMPSHIRE

Chocorua Mountain was the magnet that drew Richard Andrew and his family to vacation in the area. This splendid mountain and the lake at its foot are jewels in the crown of New Hampshire. The mountain is a bare peak about 3,500 feet high. Shelters near its top provide a place for overnight stays, a refuge dearly remembered by the thousands of climbers who experience the challenge each year.

There are many paintings by Richard Andrew of this mountain. It is one of the most photographed mountains in New England.

Oil on Canvas
16 x 20 in.
Private Collection, Richmond, Virginia

Watercolor on Paper
19 x 13 in.
Private Collection, California

Oil on Board
18 x 12 in.
Private Collection, New Hampshire

Eastern Point Lighthouse
Gloucester, Massachusetts

Oil on Board
24.75 x 20 in., 1941
Private Collection, Maine

OFF EASTERN POINT
GLOUCESTER, MASSACHUSETTS
Oil on Board
12 x 9 in.
Private Collection, Roanoke, Virginia

OLD NAHANT PIERS
Oil on Board
8.5 x 7.75 in.
Private Collection, Manchester by the Sea, Massachusetts

DRY DOCK
Oil on Canvas
21.5 x 29.5 in.
Private Collection, New Hampshire

HILL BOAT YARD, GLOUCESTER
Oil on Canvas
21 x 17 in., 1890
Private Collection, New Hampshire

THATCHER'S LIGHT

Oil on Canvas
25 x 30 in.
Courtesy of the Whistler House Museum of Art, Lowell Art Association, Inc.

RICHARD ANDREW

(1869 -1956)

Richard Andrew.

OUR STORY

From the time I can remember, Richard Andrew, or "Uncle Dick" as I called him, was part of my life. My mother and her family participated in his personal life, career, lectures, and art celebrations. His painting, "The Blueberry Girl," hung above the couch in my childhood home in Hartford, Connecticut and later in our home in upstate New York where our children learned to treasure it.

When I was a very young child, my mother took us, all five little children, to see the magnificent Hall of Valor murals painted by Richard Andrew at the Massachusetts State House in Boston. I remember how BIG they were to me, a mere six-year old. But, even then, the murals impressed me by the stories they told of war, courage, and patriotism.

Another trip left a strong impression on me. Aunt Lucy, Uncle Dick's wife, invited Mother and us children, ranging from two to seven years of age, to travel to Gloucester, Massachusetts for lunch. It must have taken courage to get us there from Hartford, Connecticut. Memory is like magic, and you never know why you remember some things and not others. But this was a very special event, I know that.

When we were about a mile from the house, Mother pulled over to an Esso gas station where there was a little bathroom on the side of the building. The three boys faces were scrubbed, hair combed just right. The baby was freshened and kissed. I was admonished not to twist the peter pan collar of my best dress.

Photograph: *Goddard children*, 1932
Ralph, Marian, Arthur, Harvey,
Betty

Marian G. Mullet, Author

We were impressed with the order expected of us, and were not exactly happy about it. We were invited into the hall that led to the kitchen of the Andrews' Cape Cod house, which we were told Uncle Dick had designed. After the women talked for awhile, it was lunch time.

We were listening for the arrival of the great Uncle Dick. Pretty soon, Aunt Lucy set the table and then proceeded to fill a tray with food. As she carried it away, she said, "Uncle Dick is painting today and will eat only when he is ready." She put the tray on a chair outside of the studio and knocked on the door three times. I was astonished, but learned a lot then and there about the drive of creative people. I was disappointed not to see him, but respectful of his right to be alone to paint original and meaningful artwork.

Years later when our granddaughter, Deb, graduated from the Rhode Island School of Design, I suggested that she and her new husband might like to visit the Massachusetts State House in Boston to see the Hall of Valor and learn about her forbearer, Richard Andrew.

Celebrating Christmas has always been a important celebration in our family. In December 2005, my husband and I climbed the steps to our daughter and her husband's home, our arms filled with Christmas gifts. We entered the kitchen to hear the murmur of family voices. We were greeted with the aroma of holiday streusel, bacon and eggs, coffee, cranberry juice, and the very special, beautifully decorated Florida pound cake.

After breakfast, as is our custom, we moved into the living room of their stately Victorian house. The Christmas tree sparkled with lights. The soft voices of the family swept over the room. One package for you and one for me, and then it was my turn. I looked at this sort of odd sized box "no, not pajamas or a sweater…Hmmm. What could it be?" Then I opened the box and could not believe my eyes. There in front of me, I discovered a portfolio of beautiful photographs of the Hall of Valor Murals and a triple matted picture of the allegorical mural panel of Joan of Arc. I was overwhelmed. Truly that gift from Deb and Dan was the most thoughtful, awe-inspiring gift I have ever received. I looked at it and exclaimed, "Now, we have to write a book about Richard Andrew, his life and achievements!"

And so we have done just that. We represent the third, fourth and fifth generations of the descendents of Richard Andrew. We determined that we would recognize, celebrate and document the life and art of this fine American artist. We could not have known then the depth of respect and love we would find for this man in the months and years to come.

We traveled the highways and byways of New England, the South, and New York to meet archivists, family members, and museum and art experts. We kept e-mails humming nationwide. We talked to and were entertained by Richard Andrew admirers. In every case, interest and support for our mission was and still is intense. There was something so inspiring in each visit, in each discussion, that we worked longer and harder to "get it right," to tell Richard Andrew's story so that you, our readers, would come to know this man and love him for the uncommon legacy he gave us.

Blueprint and photo of Richard Andrew's former studio and residence on Grapevine Road, Gloucester, Massachusetts. Photo: 2007

Over 300 heretofore unpublished paintings, portraits, landscapes, etchings, and studies have been found in our search. We saw homes graced by Andrew's paintings and owners so proud you could literally palpate their emotions.

All of us have learned about a man who touched people's hearts for more than 100 years, a man who continues to make life richer day after day for us all.

–Marian G. Mullet

Marian G. Mullet, Martha M. Winsor, Deborah W. Batt
Producers of this book, representing the third, fourth, and fifth generation descendents of Richard Andrew

About the producers of this book:

This book, produced by Marian G. Mullet, author; Martha M. Winsor, researcher and editor; and Deborah W. Batt, photographer and graphic designer, is in equal measure an experience of devotion and learning. It is with great pleasure that we fulfill the mission of telling this story to the public about an extraordinary man and his art.

Marian G. Mullet:
As Founder, President and CEO of Pathfinder Village, an international center for persons who have Down Syndrome in Edmeston, New York, the author spent thirty years writing and developing publications, fundraising proposals, and writing a book about this human service organization. Marian's forbears came from Maine and Boston. She is a nurse by profession, educated at Bates College in Lewiston, Maine, and New England Baptist Hospital in Boston. She holds honorary doctorates from Bates College and the State University of New York at Oneonta.

Martha M. Winsor:
Raised in central New York, Martha holds an undergraduate degree in art education, a Masters in Information Science, and a second Masters in Educational Administration. Her many years of experience as an administrator, researcher, and artist has given this book depth of information and clarity.

Deborah W. Batt:
Educated at Rhode Island School of Design with a Master's Degree in art education from Tufts University, Deborah teaches art and graphic design at Wakefield High School near Boston. Deborah came to this team well-equipped to provide design skills and excellent photographs. Her enthusiasm, professionalism, and artistic talents have enhanced the book each step of the way.

Bibliography

"Academie Julian." <u>AskArt: The Artists Bluebook</u>. 11 July 2006 <http://www.askart.com///_Definition.aspx?sl=E>.

Andrew, Richard. Letter to Ruth Andrew Dean. 11 Mar. 1940.

- - -. Letter to Ruth Andrew Dean. 20 Apr. 1943.

- - -. Letter to Ruth Andrew Dean. 17 Dec. 1940.

Annual of the Massachusetts Normal School of Art. "Faculty Notes." Palette and Pen (1930): 7.

- - -. "Faculty Notes." <u>Palette and Pen</u> (1925): 15.

- - -. "Faculty Notes." <u>Palette and Pen</u> (1924): 15.

- - -. "Faculty Notes." <u>Palette and Pen</u> (1921): 12.

Anonymous. Personal interview. 15 May 2006.

The Arnold Arboretum. Dept. home page. Harvard University. 4 July 2006
        <http://www.arboretum.harvard.edu//tory.html>.

"Artist Finds Perfect Joan of Arc for Model." <u>Boston Post</u> 22 May 1926: 1, 9.

"Autumn (A Decoration)." <u>Gloucester Daily Tribune</u> 16 Oct. 1913.

"Boston City Club's New Home." <u>Boston Daily</u> 7 Feb. 1915: 56. <u>ProQuest Historical Newspapers.</u> ProQuest
        Information and Learning. 12 Apr. 2007 <http://hn.bigchalk.com>.

<u>Boston Herald</u> [Boston] 4 Feb. 1934: 1, 22. <u>Massachusetts State House Lib.</u> (n.d.)

"Boston War Murals." <u>Art Digest</u> 15 Nov. 1931: 42.

Cape Ann Historical Society. "Richard Andrew." Letter to the author. 26 Apr. 2006. Cape Ann Historical Society.

Commonwealth of Massachusetts. <u>Mural Painting of the 104th Infantry, 26th Division, A.E.F. by Richard Andrew</u>.
        <u>Dedication</u>. Boston: Massachusetts State House, 1927.

- - -. Governor Alan T. Fuller. <u>Acceptance Address</u>. Boston: n.p., 1927.

"Cora Millet Holden." <u>Dittrick Medical History Center</u>. Case Western Reserve U. 12 July 2006
        <http://www.case.edu////.htm>.

"Course Calalogue." <u>College Circulars & Catalogues: Massachusetts Normal School of Art</u>. Vol. II. Copy 1. Boston:
        Massachusetts Normal School of Art, 1984.

Curl, M.J. "Boston Artists and Sculptors in Intimate Talks." <u>Boston Sunday Herald</u> 5 June 1921, sec. E: 6.

Dean, Robert C. <u>Biographical Sketches: The Forebearers of Robert Charles Dean and Ruth Andrew Dean,</u>
        <u>Second Generation</u>. Boston, Massachusetts: Benjamin Franklin Smith, 1967.

Fahey, Jeneth. "19 Grapevine Rd. Gloucester." E-mail to Martha Winsor. 9 Aug. 2006.

Falk, Peter H. "Richard Andrew." <u>Annual Exhibition Record of the Pennsylvania Academy of the Fine Arts 1876-1913</u>.
        Vol. 2. Sound View Press, 1989.

Falk, Peter Hastings, Ed. "Richard Andrew." <u>Annual Exhibition Record of the Pennsylvania Academy of Fine Arts,</u>
        <u>1914 - 1968</u>. Vol. 3. Madison, Connecticut: Sound View Press, 1969.

"The Fine Arts:Andrew's 'Girl in Black.'" <u>Boston Evening Transcript</u> 12 Mar. 1912, sec. 2: 14.

"Frederick Ryan." <u>AskArt</u>. 11 July 2001 <http://www.askart.com///_Definition.aspx?sl=R>.

Gorton's of Gloucester. "History Timeline." <u>Gorton's of Gloucester</u>. 10 Apr. 2007
        <http://www.gortons.com//_webteam.php>.

"Hall of Valor." <u>Boston Globe</u> 1 Nov. 1931: 12.

"History." <u>Guild of Boston Artists</u>. Guild of Boston Artists. 10 Apr. 2007 <http://www.guildofbostonartists.org>.

<u>Jean-Leon Gerome</u>. The Getty Museum. 10 Apr. 2007 <http://www.getty.edu///?maker=416>.

"L'Ecole des Beaux Arts." <u>AskArt: The Artists Bluebook</u>. 11 July 2006
        <http://www.askart.com///_Definition.aspx?sl=E>.

"Margaret Fitzhugh Browne." <u>Artist Biographies</u>. Lawrence J. Cantor, LC. 7 July 2006
        <http://www.fineoldart.com/_by_essay.html?essay=179>.

Massachusetts House of Representatives. <u>Bill No. 1280</u>. Boston: n.p., n.d.

Massachusetts Legislature. "19." <u>Legislative Resolution 1924</u>.

Massachusetts Normal School of Art. "Faculty Notes." Palette and Pen (1931).

Massachusetts State House. Dedication Ceremony of the 104th Infantry Regiment Murals. Boston: n.p., 1953. 37.

MassArt. "MassArt History." MassArt. 21 Mar. 2007 <http://www.massart.edu///.html>.

Michaels, David. <u>N.C. Wyeth: A Biography</u>. N.p.: Knopf, 1998.

"Modernism." <u>Ask Art: The Artists Bluebook</u>. 10 Mar. 2007 <http://www.askart.com///_Definition.aspx?sl=E>.

"Mural Painting for the State House to Honor 104th Infantry:Richard Andrew, Boston, Wins Competition."
     <u>Boston Globe</u> 15 July 1924.

"Obituary." <u>Boston Daily Globe</u> 12 July 1956: 30.

O'Hara, Frederick. "Tin Helmets and Clay Figures Inspire Great War Picture by Local Artist." <u>Boston Sunday Globe</u>
     16 Jan. 1927, sec. Editorial: 13.

"One of His Units Wins Distinction in April 1918." <u>Boston Evening Transcript</u> 5 Apr. 1924, sec. 4: 3.

"Posters for Flower Show." <u>Boston Daily Globe</u> 10 Mar. 1918. <u>ProQuest Historical Newspapers</u>. ProQuest
     Information and Learning. 12 Apr. 2007 <http://hn.bigchalk.com>.

Reynolds, Gordon. Letter to Richard Andrew. 27 May 1942. MassArt.

"Richard Andrew." <u>Annual Exhibition Record of the Art Institute of Chicago</u>, 1888-1950.

"Richard Andrew." <u>AskArt: The American Artists Bluebook</u>. 2 July 2006
     <http://www.askart.com///_Definition.aspx?sl=E>.

Sheridan, Sally Lou, and Doric Dane. Massachusetts State House. Boston: Massachusetts State House, 1994.

- - -. <u>Spelling as History</u>. Boston: Massachusetts State House, 1994.

<u>Smithsonian American Art Inventories</u>. Smithsonian Institution. 9 Mar. 2006 <http://siris-actinventories.si.edu>.
     Catalogued Inventory of the Richard Andrew murals at the Massachusetts State House

Stanley, Anna Huntington. "American Art Review." <u>History of American Art</u>. By Ingrid Swanson. 120-121.

State of Massachusetts. Governor. <u>Acceptance Address</u>. By Alan T. Fuller, Gov. Boston: n.p., 1927.

"Unveil Pictures by Boston Art Students." <u>Boston Sunday Globe</u> 19 June 1927. <u>Massachusetts State House Lib.</u> (n.d.)

"War Posters Bring Home To Patriot's Necessity of Buying Liberty Bonds." <u>Boston Daily Globe</u> 8 Apr. 1918: 9.
     <u>ProQuest Historical Newspapers</u>. ProQuest Information and Learning. 12 Apr. 2007
     <http://hn.bigchalk.com>.

W.H.D. "The Fine Arts." <u>Boston Evening Transcript</u> 29 Oct. 1918, sec. 2: 15.

- - -. "The Fine Arts: Mr. Andrew's Pictures." <u>Boston Evening Transcript</u> 29 Oct. 1918, sec. 2: 15.

- - -. "The Fine Arts: Pictures by Mr. Andrew." <u>Boston Evening Transcript</u> 16 Nov. 1920, sec. 2: 13.

LIST OF ARTWORK: